WEST SOMERSET COAST IN WATERCOLOURS

Brean to Porlock - a journey

Rosie and Howard Smith

The Garret Press

First published in the United Kingdom in November 2003.

The Garret Press, 6 Stafford Place, Weston-super-Mare, Somerset, BS23 2QZ.

British Library Cataloguing in Publication Data.

A catalogue record for this book is available from the British Library.

ISBN

0-9541546-2-2 (paperback)

0-9541546-3-0 (hardback)

Front cover illustration: Midsummer, noon, Blue Ben, St. Audrie's Bay.

Back cover: Ammonite fossil, pebbles, St Audrie's Bay.

Design: Colin Baker.

Type: 12 pt. Perpetua.

Printed in Great Britain by: R. Booth Limited, Antron Hill, Mabe, Penryn, Cornwall, TR10 9HH.

ACKNOWLEDGEMENTS

Our thanks to Kathie Barnes, Laura and Allan Hoyano, Paul Smith and Samuel Smith for reading and advising on the text. In our first book, *Weston-super-Mare in Watercolours,* our designer Colin Baker was able to realise our aspiration for a book where paintings and words were interwoven. In this sister volume we feel he has been equally successful. As before, we are grateful to David Brown for his support and guidance and to Neil Richards of Booth's for his patience and understanding.

Our gratitude is also due to the friendly advice and hospitality of Ben Norman, Jeanne and Tim Webb, Malcolm Appleton and Bill Johnson. So to, to Paul Wilson who pointed us in the right direction for people around Porlock. Thanks also to Duncan Osborne and Fred Anderson of the Rural Life Museum in Allerford, to the staff of the Tourist Information Centre in Porlock and Mike Ireland, and to Geoff Kay who gave up precious hours of a weekend to show us around Hinkley Point Nuclear Power Station. Chris Richards was, as always, very supportive - this time clearing up the mysteries of limeburning and Watchet mortar.

While we read, sketched, photographed, cycled, walked, talked and breathed the coastline for 2 years, sailing it added a fresh dimension to familiar territory. For that, we are hugely thankful to Andy and Sue Walker, their marvellous boat Goldenmean and their peerless 'seapersonship.' Without them we might never have seen the Gore buoy.

Thanks as well to Holger and Karin Schneeweiss who found my camera at the top of Hurlstone Combe and made sure it came back to me.

This book is dedicated to Andy and Sue Walker.

INTRODUCTION

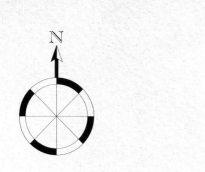

West Somerset Coast

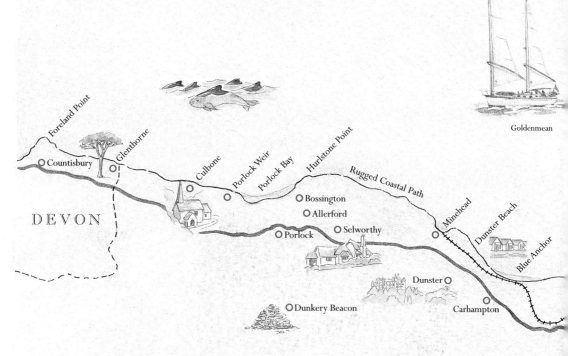

Aberthaw

Goldenmean

Foreland Point

Glenthorne

Countisbury

DEVON

Culbone

Porlock Weir

Porlock Bay

Hurlstone Point

Rugged Coastal Path

Bossington

Allerford

Porlock

Selworthy

Minehead

Dunster Beach

Blue Anchor

Dunkery Beacon

Dunster

Carhampton

Roadw

Exmoor National Park

BRENDON HILLS

SOMERSET

| 0 | 1 | 2 | 3 | 4 | 5 Miles |
| 0 | 1 | 2 | 3 | 4 | 5 | 6 | 7 Kilometres |

Penarth ○

Barry ○

Flat Holm

Steep Holm

Sand Point

Sand Bay

Worlebury

Weston-super-Mare ○

Brean Down

Bleadon Hill

Brean

Bridgwater Bay

Wreck
of the
'Nornen'

Berrow

Brent Knoll

A370

Gore buoy

Hinkley Point

Stolford

Steart

Burnham-on-Sea ○

A38

Highbridge ○

River Brue

East Quantoxhead

Kilve Beach

Lilstock

St. Audrie's
Bay

○ Kilton

○ Stogursey

Combwich ○

River Parrett

Doniford ○

○ Kilve

Williton

○ West
Quantoxhead

Holford ○

Nether Stowey ○

A39

Bridgwater ○

QUANTOCK HILLS

gumber ○

Crowcombe Heathfield ○

Burrow Mump ○

Bishops Lydeard ○

INTRODUCTION

View from Bleadon Hill

In our first book *Weston-super-Mare in Watercolours,* Rosie and I describe the Somerset coastline in the vicinity of our home town, taking in three Bristol Channel promontories: Sand Point, Worlebury and Brean Down. The success of that book has inspired this attempt to depict the rest of the Somerset coast in a similar way, a combination of personal narrative and intimate watercolours. We intend this book to be the second of three, taking in the entire Somerset seaboard.

A few years ago I bought an 1809 edition Ordnance Survey map[1] showing the Somerset coastline from Sand Point (just north of Weston-super-Mare) to the Somerset - Devon border at 'Coscomb Bay' (sic), about 4 miles (6.5 km) west of Porlock. With its scale of 1 inch : 1 mile, it has provided a fascinating insight into what was on the ground 200 years ago. Another enjoyable source has been Charles Harper's book *The Somerset Coast* published in 1909. He had a droll and, at times, acerbic view of all the changes the countryside was experiencing at the beginning of the 20th century. In some ways, he has been a travelling companion and I have dropped in his comments along the way.

[1] *Published Oct. 11th 1809 by Lt. Col. Mudge; Tower and Engraved at the Drawing Room in the Tower by Benjamin Baker and Assistants.*

So, in these pages, we journey south: from Brean Down to the River Parrett estuary and then sharp west, along a coast of many colours, to Porlock Weir. The journey closes at the Somerset - Devon border, where it runs up the wooded ravine of Coscombe, west of Sugarloaf Hill on Exmoor, above Glenthorne Beach. We have walked the whole way, and we have sailed it on three occasions with Andy and Sue Walker, on their good ship 'Goldenmean.'[2] Rosie has sketched a number of 'views from the boat', in the spirit of 19th century Royal Navy survey drawings. As in the previous book, I have added 'Special Pages' and footnotes providing more information and stories on particular subjects that have intrigued us.

Bridgwater Bay and its bordering country is familiar territory to both of us. My parents took me, my sister and two brothers, on many a 'Sunday run' to Brean sands, the Quantocks or Minehead. In my teens I hauled my loaded BSA bike along the A39 road to camp at Holford and explore the beaches at Kilve. Rosie's introduction was a touch more cerebral. She attended school study weeks at Holford's Combe House Hotel and Kilve Court run by Somerset County Council. But although much was familiar, our journeyings for the book turned out to have more than their share of discovery and surprise.

Approaching Weston-super-Mare along the West Mendip Way, with Crook's Peak peering over our shoulders, at the summit of Bleadon Hill there is a moment when the Somerset coastline fills the view with a panoramic sweep north, south and west. Broken stone walls and wind-blown hawthorn occupy the foreground with a grove of beech, oak and Scots pine. To the right, the treeline crumples down Hutton Hill into Hay Wood. There, with Uphill hidden away below the hill, a foreshortened Brean Down hunkers at the sea's edge ready to pounce on a Steep Holm sitting nonchalantly mid-channel. Away to our left Brean and Berrow sands form an unbroken southward swerve until they meet the estuaries of the Rivers Parrett and Brue.

[2] *'Goldenmean' is a 'Nereus', 40' Cat Ketch, designed by Mark Ellis Design Ltd. of Oakville, Ontario, Canada. Her two masts (47' & 43') are unstayed with wishbone rigs - similar to a windsurfer.*

Then, as though undergoing a sudden change of plan, the shore makes a right angle, travelling west across the coastal levels of Stert Flats, past the silent towers of Hinkley Point, to meet the Quantock and Exmoor seaboard. About here (from where we are standing up on Bleadon Hill) the coastline begins to lose definition and folds away in a series of headlands with Foreland Point demarcating the Somerset - Devon border, 2.5 miles (4 km) west of the Somerset county line. The Severn Sea continues on beyond the horizon to meet the Atlantic Ocean and the Western Approaches.

Goldenmean

Chapter One

BLEADON, BREAN AND BERROW

St. Peter's Church, Bleadon

The prospect from Bleadon Hill provides a magnificent overview of the whole south and west Somerset coast. But for all that, you can scarcely see Bleadon Village - just the top third of the Perpendicular tower of St.Peter's Church, as it peeks above the brow of the hill. If you continue on along the West Mendip Way, from Roman Road there are several footpaths[3] which lead down the hillside fields into the village, all with the glint of the sea in the west. Bleadon is comfortably sheltered on the southern side of the Mendip Hills with a fine pub 'The Queens Arms' (where I could get a pint of Flowers beer, even in the dead-ale days of Watney's Red Barrel) and a really delightful association of church, village cross[4] and post office - unchanged from drawings of 100 years ago. The name of the village may have arisen from a bloody slaughter of Viking invaders by the locals - Bleed-down.[5] Academics will have none of it, although they haven't come up with anything better. The village is defended from the A370 by wide fields and rhynes and one road runs on, past the defunct quarries of the South Hill, to join the A370 main road where it crosses the River Axe at Bleadon Bridge. The other (Bleadon Road) passes back along the footings of the hillside to meet the same A370 a little further north, opposite The Anchor Inn on Accommodation Road.

[3]*One ends in the small hamlet of Wonderstone, possibly named after a beautiful limestone found near by -*
"yellow transparent crystals distributed through a dark red earthy dolomite."

[4]*For many years the cross went 'missing' although everyone in the village seemed to know where it was.*
In 1929 a newly arrived Rector heard that it had been 'adapted' as a horse hitching post in a nearby farm.
He eventually found it propping up a roost in a hen house.

[5]*My Aunty Jean, newly arrived from Hastings just before the war, started work as a clerk for a*
firm of solicitors in Weston. On her first day she was asked by one of the senior partners "to fetch the Bleadon files."
To the horror of her fellow workers, my aunt replied "Which bleeding files?"
But then she was from Hastings and knowing Aunty Jean....

Accommodation Road appears never to know exactly where it's going. It's supposed to go to Brean but after a few twists it promptly heads off in the opposite direction and, for a while, seems to be curving back to the main road. But bear with it, follow the signs for Brean and Berrow and it'll get you there in the end. The reason for its inebriated journey is that the railway (which it crosses 3 times) and the River Axe (once) keep getting in the way. Coming from Weston, you can bypass some of this by taking the Walborough foot and cycle path from Uphill. At one time the Axe may have been navigable as far as Axbridge, but in 1841 the railway put an end to most of the river traffic. Until the 1940s, boats still unloaded coal at Lympsham Wharf (Wharf Farm today) close to Accommodation Road.

View of Brent Knoll

This is Level land. Rich pasture, drained by a network of rhynes and ditches which has always been vulnerable to flood. The rhynes are lined with the waving wands of the Common Reed whose flowering heads start off a dark purple brown and, in autumn, change into greyish downy plumes. Even in winter, when the seed-down has blown away, they wave on, softening the windy landscape. Accommodation Road is home to high brambles and the blackberries are sweet and plentiful. Along the road are beautiful farmhouses, many built of a soft terracotta brick that may have come from the brickyards of Uphill or Highbridge. Hope Farm, sitting on one of the road's many right angles, about a mile west of Lympsham, is a fine example. It sits back from the road on wide lawns which allow its light Gothic style[6] to breath freely. Along the garden's western border runs a rhyne overlooked by a magnificent horsechestnut.

Apple Orchard, Dobunni Fruit Farm

[6]*Lympsham has a large number of houses and farm buildings which were built in the Gothic style during the latter half of the 19th century. The local landowner and rector Joseph Henry Stephenson was quite ruthless in imposing his preferred designs on the community.*

A little further on from Hope Farm is Dobunni Fruit Farm where fine Somerset cider is made, from sweet to scrumpy. The farm also grows dessert apples; Rosie and I rediscovered the sweet, scented, flavour of a newly picked Worcester and the wonderful, mouthfilling, acidic crunch of the James Grieve apple. Dobunni is part of a 'Cider Renaissance', and this is especially true in Somerset where there are more small cider-makers than in any other county. Ian and Brenda Gibson have been replanting trees on the Lympsham levels since the mid-1980s and the manicured orchards are a testament to their enthusiasm.

It has to be admitted that reaching Brean is a bit of a disappointment. Where is the sea? It was always hidden behind high sand dunes of course, but the bungalows that now cap those dunes seem to present an impenetrable barrier - although I can forgive the sugar-icing confection of one called 'The Castle.' There have been caravans here for years and that's fair enough I suppose, but these days they're reproducing at an unstoppable rate! 'Mobile' homes are moving in too. What is a real shame are the ones on the narrow fields close to the sea-wall at the northern end of the beach road. They completely obscure the view of Brean Down from the road, which should be an imposing sight. Nowadays that sense of drama can only be recaptured by walking along the beach. Thankfully The National Trust have acquired most of the Down.[7] Perhaps one day they'll get hold of some its hinterland so the peninsula can be seen in its proper setting once again. Ironically Brean Down is far more visible from Weston even though it belongs to Brean.

[7] And thanks too to William Wyndham and his restrictive covenants for selling it to Axbridge Council for a bargain price.

Brean Down is the big brother of three conspicuous promontories on this part of the Somerset coast. The other two are Worlebury Hill[8] and Sand Point. On its south side it projects about 1.5 miles (2.4 km) into the sea and rises to a height of 321 ft (100 m). Viewed from the beach, the Down is massive and dramatic. The south cliffs, sheer and intimidating, are recognised in rock climbing circles and are best left to experts. You may come across a goat[9] or two perched on a dizzying ledge - dogs don't fare so well, toppling from the heights at the rate of one a month.

[8]*Worlebury is wooded because the Lord of the Manor decided he wanted a woodland 'game preserve' in the early 19th century.*

[9]*A herd of wild goats has become established on the Down over the past 20 years. One winter's day I came across over 15 of them eying me with suspicion from rocky crags above the southern cliffs.*

The Down presents a wide range of wildlife habitats and the grassy downland is kept that way through the dental activity of cattle, sheep and rabbits. Along the north side, which has a shelving gradient, hawthorn, bramble and bracken[10] proliferate, providing good cover for small birds. The southern cliff-faces are windy and exposed but they also receive the full heat of the sun. Here wild thyme and the rare white rock-rose thrive and, in late May, the southern side can be covered with the white bloom of the rock-rose - "as though it had been sprinkled with salt." Brean Down is one of very few place in Britain where the white species (Helianthemum appeninium) grows. And it's doing very well! In the stony crevices where the sun warms, rock samphire grows freely. Around the promontory's tip, samphire's succulent leaves can be found in great abundance - at one time it was collected and pickled, a risky job with a good deal of 'falling off' involved. Shakespeare describes it as a 'dreadful trade' in King Lear.

White rock rose

[10]*Bracken is a fern that only does well on acidic soil. Brean Down is mainly Carboniferous limestone which is alkaline. The bracken is growing on a layer of acid soil left by an ancient glacier. It can be poisonous to animals which is why they avoid it and another reason it's growing so well here.*

Brean Down searchlight post

These days access to the Down is from the south side - the small ferry which used to ply the River Axe during summer on the Weston-super-Mare side, has long been forsaken. There is a circuit walk which starts close to the beach and ascends a steep stairway to gain the crest of the peninsula. A gentler way up is along the old military road which travels to the landward end of the Down. The outlook from the top is breathtaking with the wide sweep of Weston Bay to the north, the Victorian town pressed up against Worlebury Hill. To the south Brent Knoll, and the flat arc of Bridgwater Bay curving to the Quantocks. Looking back to the east, the Mendips stretch away beyond Bleadon Hill and Crook's Peak. In the far distance Glastonbury Tor stands clear of the misty levels, while all about is the Severn Sea with its islands, and Wales following the west horizon.

At the end of Brean Down stand the remains of a Victorian fort constructed in 1860s to resist French invasion. It linked up with similar gun batteries on Steep Holm, Flat Holm and Lavernock Point in Wales. In 1900 Gunner Haines blew himself up and quite a bit of the fort, by firing a carbine into an ammunition magazine. He was judged to be 'in a state of temporary insanity.' There wasn't too much left of poor Gunner Haines, but a skull was found some years later, by a picnicking party, in a spot where his head might have arrived. They threw it into the sea in horror. The defences were reinstituted during the Second World War and the searchlight post at the end of the Down looks to Steep Holm where a sister light also shone across the water. The National Trust has recently restored much of the fort, though for safety reasons it is now rather sanitised - access to the underground magazines is blocked by strong steel grills.

After taking the western path out to the fort, the way back along the old military road has a cosier atmosphere. The scrub here has to be cut back from time to time, or the grassland would be overwhelmed, but it does provide cover for birds such as whitethroats and linnets, both delightful musicians. The bumpy road curves south at the Down's east end and the viewpoint here reveals the twisting course of the River Axe[11] and Old Uphill Church standing roofless on its quarried cliff.

[11]The subterranean source of the River Axe arises from a cave at the entrance to the Cheddar Gorge and, on the other side of Crook's Peak, from energetic springs near Winscombe (which form the Lox Yeo River).

Brean is now very much a holiday place. When I was a child it seemed a remote village involving quite a long journey from Weston. The beach and sands went on for ever and the lowering cliffs of the Down were slightly scary.[12] Camping had become popular in the fields along the coast road in the 1930s - the dry, sandy soil was perfect for pitching a tent. Then redundant buses began to arrive, to be converted into holiday homes on small plots of land. Much of this was uncontrolled and explains why a lot of the Brean and Berrow foreshore is in private hands. In 1935 a holiday camp with wooden sheds for 300 people was established by Leslie Dean. Taken over by the Army during the war, it was pretty well wrecked, but in 1947 Fred Pontin from Bristol took it over and it became the first Pontin Holiday Camp.

Sarah on Berrow sands

[12]*One day my family arrived at Brean for a picnic and a swim. This included me carrying a huge,
red inflated, tractor inner-tube which I had tested on the Marine Lake in Weston. Anyway the tide was in!
So I splashed about a bit and was feeling pretty pleased with myself, until I suddenly noticed the shore
was rather a long way off. The wind was skimming me out to sea. I could hardly reach down over the sides
of the tube to paddle, so there was a good deal of panicky flapping about. I did eventually make it back,
or I might never have been writing this. Lost at sea, on a huge red inner-tube.....*

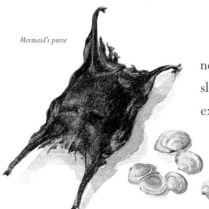

Mermaid's purse

Tellin shells

Brean and Berrow Sands sweep firm and wide for nearly six miles. Like Weston they are great for slogging a cricket ball vast distances, fielders becoming exhausted specks disappearing into the haze. Sand yachting has become established and at low tide the great expanse of sand allows plenty of freedom for the sport. Years ago, horses and greyhounds were raced at organised meets. Horse riding remains hugely popular - understandable with the opportunity to gallop along the tidal margin for mile after mile. In its winter season, sea angling for the likes of codling, cod,[13] whiting and dab is avidly pursued - often competitively. There is reasonable footpath access from the coast road, and you can walk the full distance along the beach, from Brean to Berrow and Burnham, with no more interruption than stepping across the occasional streamlet threading its way over the sands. The high dunes isolate you from the low lying Somerset levels to the east and, at the Brean end, the foreshore bungalows have erected palisades to defend themselves from trippers and wind blown sand.

Eventually the developed foreshore gives way to the Berrow Dunes;[14] a Local Nature Reserve and a Site of Special Scientific Interest and, with hindsight, this is how all this stretch of coastline should have been protected.

[13] *At 6pm on the 18th December 2002, a frosty evening with a south-west breeze and a calm sea, a good friend of mine, Chris Clarke, caught a huge 26lb 10oz cod (12.4kg) on the Berrow Sands. This was reckoned to be possibly the heaviest cod ever taken from the shore along the Somerset coast. A few days later his companion, Ian Clark, landed a 21lb 12oz specimen (9.8kg) close by! The Berrow Sands became a trifle busy after that.*

[14] *The dunes (or 'tots' as they are called locally) are in a state of constant change with the wind breaking through and making gaps (blowouts) which allow fresh sand movement - this encourages the growth of Marram grass which will stabilise the dunes once again. Strangely Marram grass only thrives in fresh sand.*

As a result the reserve is rich in wildlife and especially so where fixed dune grassland has become established. Immediately south, just where the tower of St. Mary's Church peeks above the Berrow Dunes, lies the Burnham and Berrow Golf Links[15] providing a pleasant, undulating, sward. On its seaward side the links are bounded by reed choked wetland which the footpath has to cross on a raised wooden walkway. St. Mary's Church[16] is tucked down below the raised shoreline and has been here since at least the 13th century. Since that time the surrounding land has risen so that the church occupies its own small dell. Inside, a dazzling west-facing vestry window catches the afternoon and evening light - from under black clouds a dark sailing ship rides on a sparkling green-blue sea towards a sun filled sky.[17]

[15]*The golf links, founded in 1890, were not popular with the Berrow folk at first and there were various attempts at sabotage - the greens were dug up and horses tethered on them. It took a few years for the villagers to come round and not feel threatened, but the club provided valuable work and in time the 'boys' and caddies became successful professional golfers themselves.*

[16]*St. Bridget's, St. Mary's sister church in Brean, is also close to the shore and was probably founded by Irish monks. Its name is rare in Somerset. Like Berrow it's a small church - underlining the two villages' poverty over the centuries. In 1703 St. Bridget's tower was struck by lightning and then badly damaged in the great storm of 1729 - it may not have been well repaired. It was replaced with the small roofed tower of today.*

[17]*'The Ship Window' was crafted in 1970 by J. Bell and Son to the design of Geoffrey A. K. Robinson. It is in memory of Janet Mercie Hitchin 1879 - 1968.*

Back on the beach, slightly north-west of the church and at low tide, the black skeletal remains of a sailing ship curve up and out of the sands. This is all that is left of the 'Nornen', grounded on the Berrow Flats in 1897.[18] From here the shore drifts south-east and after 2 miles (3.2 km) we come to Burnham-on-Sea. The boundary between Berrow and Burnham has moved about but, with house building along the coastal road, the village now blurs imperceptibly into the town.

The Wreck of the 'Nornen'

[18] *In a storm of wind and snow, 'Nornen' had broken anchors off Lundy Island and was eventually driven ashore at Berrow. The Burnham lifeboat 'John Godfrey Morris' transferred the crew (and the ship's dog) to shore amidst crashing waves.*
But the 'Nornen' couldn't be refloated and was dissembled on the sands leaving the shattered hulk to the tides. Her figurehead now rests in the Village Hall.
At the time of writing, after a hundred years, the wreck has suddenly become 'a hazard' and the District Council is making moves to remove it! Good Grief!

   Gazing out over all this low land, about 3 miles (4.8 km) back from the coast,
is the flat topped hill of Brent Knoll. It rises more than 450 ft (137 m) above the plain,
striking because it stands so clear of any other high ground.[19] From the sea it is a
conspicuous landmark - as it is from the M5 motorway, which respectfully curves in
accommodation as it passes to the east. Around its summit are the remains of an Iron-
age hill-fort (like Worlebury) with evidence that it later served as a Roman hill station.
At some stage Lias stone was quarried from the top of the hill. A road runs round the
circumference of the knoll linking the villages of East Brent to the north-east, and Brent
Knoll to the south-west. St. Mary's Church in East Brent has a beautiful, unrestored,
15th century spire in a lovely setting on the side of the hill. 180 degrees away to the
south stands St. Michael's Church in Brent Knoll village. Also finely placed on the
hillside but looking to the sea, the church has a Perpendicular tower and is famous for
some medieval bench-ends which, with almost a cartoon-like quality, illustrate the
demise of a fox dressed as a bishop, descending from his pomp to the stocks and ending
up hanged! Strong stuff, and just who were 'they' getting at?

[19]*It's interesting that Glastonbury Tor, to which the Knoll has a strong resemblance, is made up of similar Lias
clays and limestones. Just why these isolated hills were resistant to the erosion of ancient seas is unclear.*

Chapter Two

BURNHAM-ON-SEA

The Lower Light

Just two miles south
of the wreck of the
'Nornen,' and standing
36 feet (11 m) above the
sands on nine wooden
stilts, is the smaller
of Burnham's two
lighthouses. Known as
'the lower light', it has
the appearance of a large
wooden lantern - which,

I suppose, is just what it is. 500 yards (450 m)
inland and slightly to the north-east, peering over trees and
roofs, is 'the higher light.' It looks like a proper lighthouse and rises 90 ft (27 m) above
high water, though curiously out of place, in a Monty Python sort of way, in its
suburban setting.[20] Both lights have a wide red line down their seaward aspect so when
the lines or the lights align, a ship at sea can calculate the correct position for safe entry
into the River Parrett.[21] The lamp of the lower light was turned off in 1969 by Trinity
House but has recently been reinstated by the district council. The higher light, now
part of a private house, shines no more.

[20]*While travelling down the Berrow to Burnham Road our 4 year old granddaughter Sarah caught sight of the*
higher lighthouse for the first time. "How did that get there!?" she cried - and she's right.
The lighthouse is always a surprise when you're going along the Berrow Road.

[21]*The lights were built in the 1830s, but within a few years the moving banks of the Parrett meant the alignment*
was not reliable. This area of the Somerset coast was always hazardous with drowned seamen often cast up
on the Gore Sands. There is a local tale that, in the mid-1700s, a fisherman's wife placed a candle in the window
of their cottage near the church, to guide him home. Not only he, but his fellow fishermen came to rely on that light.
Some years later the church sexton had a powerful light shine from the church tower which overlooked the sea.
This was taken over by the Rev. David Davies who erected a tower-beacon next to the church (the castellated
stump of that first lighthouse, known as The Round Tower, still stands). All this eventually provoked Trinity House
(the governing agency) into erecting the upper and lower lighthouses and the Rev. Davies was paid the tidy sum of
£13,681 - just a bit more than the £5 the fisherman's wife had received from the sexton!

In the 1830s, looking to the explosive development of Weston-super-Mare, a Reverend David Davies decided that Burnham should get in on the action. He 'discovered' some mineral springs but the tastings were not a success; *"The water was turbid and slightly yellow. The smell was very offensive, resembling that of a cesspool, mixed with an odour not unlike bad horseradish."* Well he wasn't going to get far with that! But he did try - building a Bath House[22] on the esplanade to accommodate the waters, but interest soon petered out. All the same, Burnham gently grew into a small seaside resort. In 1858 the town received an extension of the Somerset Central Railway from Highbridge, which ran to a landing-slip on the seafront. The jetty linked Burnham with other seaside towns on the Bristol Channel but was eventually thwarted by river siltage. The remains of the jetty still reach out into the sea from the Esplanade, opposite Pier Street.

No. 2 buoy, off Burnham sands

[22]*Sea water was pumped into the basement where the baths were located. The waters were said to be "Good for relieving obstinate complaints of the stomach, bowels, obstruction of the liver, bilious affections, debility and wasting of the limbs and frame...."*

For centuries people along the low-lying Somerset coast, between Burnham and Clevedon, had had to deal with flood. Elaborate drainage systems were devised with raised river banks extending for miles inland combined with rhynes and dykes around the fields. Flood waters are usually produced by a combination of forces: high tides and onshore gales with heavy rain falling on the high ground to the east. In 1606 the floods were devastating and extended from the coast to Glastonbury - a distance of over 15 miles (24 km). An etching from the time shows water lapping church roofs, people in trees, sitting on house tops or swimming in all directions with cattle, goats and sheep. There is even a baby in a crib bobbing amongst the confusion.

Events repeated themselves down the years with varying severity, but in December 1981 the sea broke through with tremendous force. The sea-wall and promenade in Weston-super-Mare were smashed and flood water poured into Uphill, Brean, Berrow, Burnham and beyond. Indeed, up to 1911 when the first Burnham sea-wall was built, sea-defences were almost non-existent and the buildings along the Esplanade must have been very vulnerable. The 1981 experience, in which a substantial area of the town

Burnham sea-front

was under water, led to the construction of the new sea-wall in 1988. The wall stretches from just beyond the lane Maddox Slade in the north to the estuary of the River Brue in the south. It is an uncompromisingly modern structure (it won the approval of The Concrete Society) which at the same time is sympathetic to the 19th century character of the seafront. Broken stone panels relieve the severity of the concrete, and stainless steel railings impart a reassuring feeling of high quality. On the seaward side, the swooping concave arc gives the wall a dramatic presence - a mirror image of a wave about to break - its height reinforced by the steps up from the beach.

The sea-wall at Burnham

It's good to see a Forte's still survives in Pier Street. There used to be many of these Italian ice-cream 'parlors' in the Somerset seaside towns, brewing coffee and making their own wonderful ice-cream. Weston's three representatives have long gone, but there are still family-run Forte's in Clevedon and in Cheddar, both doing good trade.

St. Andrew's Church stands back from the seafront with grounds that slope up to the Esplanade - an indication of the former protective sand dunes I suspect. Its tower has a slightly disturbing lean[23] and inside, in various parts of the building, are bits of an altar piece that used to reside in the chapel of Whitehall Palace, originally commissioned by King James the Second in 1686. As you enter the church grounds from the Esplanade, looking north, you can see The Round Tower (behind Marine House, no.43a) - the truncated remains of Burnham's first lighthouse (see preceding footnote).

[23]*Lympsham church tower also tilts although the topmost pinnacles return to the vertical. This gives the tower an unsettling kink which makes you wonder if you're seeing it quite right.*

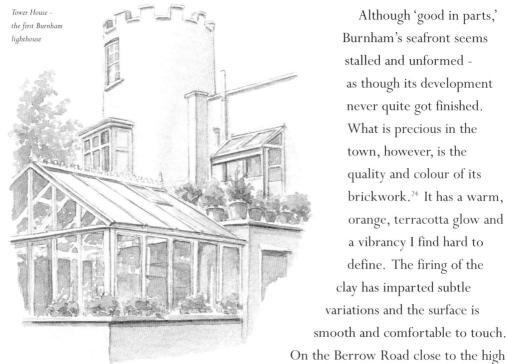

Tower House - the first Burnham lighthouse

Although 'good in parts,' Burnham's seafront seems stalled and unformed - as though its development never quite got finished. What is precious in the town, however, is the quality and colour of its brickwork.[24] It has a warm, orange, terracotta glow and a vibrancy I find hard to define. The firing of the clay has imparted subtle variations and the surface is smooth and comfortable to touch. On the Berrow Road close to the high lighthouse, behind a tall Gothic gateway and expansive lawns stand Ellen's Cottages.[25] This single storey terrace has three grand porches and walls of soft orange brick. There is curved Bath stone detailing around the doorways and windows, all unified by a steep slate roof. Burnham brick also finds its way into many of the later Victorian and Edwardian villas in this part of the town - which, with its successful tennis and golf clubs and wide leafy roads, breathes an atmosphere of comfortable well-being. Ben Travers, whose farces were so successful during the 1960s and 70s, lived in a house at the entrance to The Grove from the Berrow Road. He gently lampooned Burnham in his play 'Rookery Nook' - his home town appearing in thin disguise as Clumpton-on-Sea.

[24]*During the 19th century Burnham boasted several brickyards of its own, but there can be little doubt that some of the bricks used in the town's buildings came from yards in Highbridge and Bridgwater.*

[25]*'Ellen's Cottages' were built in 1838 by John Saunders in memory of his wife. They were to be taken by "ten poor women". Being so close to the lighthouse, it's easy to imagine that some of them might have been occupied by the widows of men lost at sea.*

At the top of Victoria Street, immediately behind St. Andrew's church, is a small brick building with two small quatrefoil windows and a central doorway that appears to have found its way from a garden shed. To one side are some stone mounting steps and, just above one of the windows, a sign indicating; 'No unauthorised parking at any time' and another stating; 'Vicar's Parking.' Divine rights? At Christmas this is home to a delightful Nativity Scene. A little further south, at the junction of Victoria Street and Princess Street, stands 'The Victoria Hotel' which appears to have been formed from two early Victorian houses. On its end wall in Princess Street is what looks like small old shop front complete with fascia-board - the off-licence perhaps? The High Street has retained a busy local personality and on its landward side are several small terraces. These superb brick cottages (eg. South Terrace) are beautifully detailed with white painted gables and the occasional bay window.

Divine parking rights

Looking west from the mouth of the River Brue

The Somerfield supermarket, which abuts the Esplanade towards its southern end, should have known better. The way it turns its back on the promenade behind a bleak car park is bad mannered and its yellow reconstituted stone block-work has nothing to do with Burnham. Unfortunately similar yellow 'stone' has also been used in new buildings along the promenade - including the Tourist Information Centre! The tamarisk hedge does soften the frontage a little, but additional sympathetic landscaping would help a lot. Compared with the town's brick buildings, the row of square aluminium windowed houses that stretch along the South Esplanade appear insipid. The sea frontage just evaporates. Their modernity should not have precluded the use of local materials which would have reinforced a Burnham identity.

South Esplanade and its promenade run out at the mouth of the River Brue, just where the small river shares estuaries with the River Parrett. Here the sea-wall curves back, high above the river; a fine position to watch the comings and goings of yachts and boats as they negotiate the difficult entrance into the Brue. You can see to the flat land of Stert Island, then across the Parrett mouth to Stert Point and the isolated community of Steart.[26] It's here that the coastline makes a right angled turn westwards and your eyes are drawn, ineluctably, to the square and arresting, grey towers of Hinkley Point Nuclear Power Station, six miles off, across the Stert Flats, beyond Stolford.

[26] *Why some parts are 'Stert' and others 'Steart' appears to be just another Somerset idiosyncrasy - although they are pronounced differently! Whichever; the word appears to derive from the Anglo-Saxon 'steort' meaning a projection of land 'starting' out to sea.*

The Sea Sketches

Emerging from the Brue estuary, off Burnham sands, in Andy and Sue Walker's ketch 'Goldenmean.' It's 8am and we have caught the top of the tide so, as it falls, the current will bear us westward down the Somerset coast. The boat's two great windsurfer sails will gather every bit of wind that's going.

Chapter Three

TWO RIVERS

Boats on the Brue

The River Brue has always played a subsidiary role to the Parrett and indeed it only just escapes being a tributary. The channel, from the river into the sea, follows a convulsive twist - so negotiating a route between the mud-banks requires a good deal of local knowledge. Despite these difficulties, the Brue has a thriving yacht club - the Burnham-on-Sea Yacht Club - which has recently installed floating pontoon moorings[27] on the river-margin below the southern end of the town's sea-wall. These rise and fall with the river/sea level allowing the wooden gangways to stay mud free and safe at all states of the tide.

[27] The cylindrical, steel, uprights have been driven deep into the river bed. They should have gone further but were halted by the bedrock of Blue lias. At low water they appear ludicrously high above the moored boats, but this is the Severn Sea, with a tidal rise and fall exceeded only by the Bay of Fundy in Eastern Canada. With a big spring tide (up to 39 ft / 12m in Burnham) and an onshore wind, the river can spill over its banks, the moored boats then floating only 12 ft (3.7m) from, and their masts well clear of, the top of the steel poles.

The path, on the north side of the Brue, runs along the raised bank high above the river and adjoining land. It continues, with a few turns, behind a boatyard (the original pill or harbour) and on into Highbridge. If it wasn't for the main road (A38) running through its heart, the buildings in the town's centre would form an attractive group, for many are of the warm local brick. Up to the mid-19th century Highbridge was a small hamlet. The main reason for its existence, and what gave it its name, is the crossing it provided over the River Brue. The same river allowed access to the sea. The construction of Highbridge Wharf and the arrival of the railway (both the 'Bristol & Exeter' and the 'Somerset & Dorset' railway companies) changed things completely. Brickyards expanded and railway workshops were established - Highbridge[28] became a place of rude industry, quite distinct in character from its sister town, Burnham, which was striving for gentility!

[28]*Charles Harper, in 1909, never comfortable with the encroaching mechanised world, considered Highbridge "forlorn and abject" and the town's railway men as " - a large and offensive, and exceptionally blackguardly colony. Radicals and Socialists to a man..."*

Admiral Blake

Robert Blake was born in Bridgwater in 1598. His father Humphrey was a successful ship owner, and a seaman in one of his boats was amongst the first to spot the Spanish Armada in the English Channel. Blake left Bridgwater to attend Wadham College in Oxford (a Somerset family foundation), after which he entered the family business in Plymouth, returning to Bridgwater - just in time for the Civil War. He became a Lieutenant Colonel on the Parliamentary side, outstanding in many West Country battles and sieges, both in defence and in attack. After the mainland defeat of the Royalist army, Blake was given the job of mopping up the Royal Fleet. He became one of three 'Generals at Sea', responsible for the reorganisation of the Navy and introducing a system of promotion through merit. From 1648 to his death in 1657, Blake was involved in many sea battles with the Dutch Fleet and a certain Lieutenant Admiral Tromp. Blake was badly injured in 1653 fighting the Dutch in the Channel and he never fully recovered. His final and greatest triumph came in April 1657 when he defeated the Spanish fleet at The Battle of Tenerife. At last Cromwell ordered Blake home to recuperate, but during the journey he became gravely ill, dying within a few hours of Plymouth Sound. Robert Blake kept close contact with Bridgwater throughout his illustrious career and was highly regarded by both enemy and friend. He never married. He was buried in Westminster Abbey, but with the restitution of the monarchy his remains were disinterred and thrown into a pit sited in common ground close by.

The main road remains a disruptive presence, though much quieter these days with the motorway to the east. Turning down Clyce Road, just south of the Highbridge Inn, a walk of 400 yards (366 m) brings you to the Highbridge Clyce.[29] Built from huge, rather alien, blocks of flecked granite, it forms a twin arched bridge across the Brue, with each arch carrying a pair of hydraulically controlled sluice-gates. From the clyce bridge you can look down the course of the river towards Burnham, the tops of the yacht club mooring poles just visible in the distance. Clyce Road follows the northern tree filled bank of the river. On the opposite side of the road are stretched out terraces of two storey artisan cottages with names like - 'Island Cottages' (1877), and a touch grander, 'Florence Villas' (1909) with a cast-iron porch. In many the wonderful brickwork has been lost under crude render, but in some, this is being painstakingly chipped away. When I was passing, I even saw uPVC windows being dumped and in their stead, new wooden sash replacements. Hallelujah!

The Highbridge Clyce

[29]*Clyce is a Somerset word for a tidal dam. When the water table is high after heavy rain, the clyce is opened at low tide so that the land can drain into the sea. The clyce may then be closed at high tide so that tidal water does not resaturate the land. When the land is dry and drainage needs to be discouraged, a clyce can be kept closed at all states of the tide.*

These days Highbridge has fused with Burnham and housing has filled the space between them. On the A38 they are even bound together on the same town sign.

Victorian villa, Clyce Road, Highbridge

South of the Brue, the land bounding the eastern banks of the Parrett continues flat and level until it encounters the moderate rise of Pawlett Hill. The A38 skids past Pawlett village ('Pollitt' to the locals) whose new houses adorn the hill crest as you approach it from the north. From the hill's summit - a little way along Gaunts Road - you can see over the Pawlett Hams;[30] pastures almost encircled by a 300 degree turn of the Parrett as it curls its slow way from Bridgwater. On the opposite bank of the river the old port of Combwich sits below its sister village of Otterhampton and the rising ground of the Quantock Hills. A ferry used to run between Combwich and the Pawlett side and the old ferry-way[31] is still there, demarcated by a tarmacked path called White House Road. A whitewashed building, The White House Inn, once stood close to the Pawlett bank - all that's left is a stone garden wall surrounding dilapidated sheds, a lapsed caravan and a shattered Cypress tree. More of this a bit further on.

The site of
'The White House Inn'

[30]*A 'ham' is an old English term for pasture or meadow, often surrounded or enclosed by a ditch.*
The Pawlett Hams were reckoned to be amongst the richest pasture in the West Country.
Flooding two or three times a year would deposit enriching silt over the land.

[31]*Stagecoaches used to come this way with travellers changing to a fresh team after they had crossed the river. There is a story that on a wild night a coach and horses, frightened by a crash of thunder, bolted and in the dark and confusion veered past the White House Inn and down into black depths of the Parrett, never to be seen again. 'Tis said, there are times when the sound of wheels, hooves and the screams of the passengers, can be heard through the river-mist...*

At the bottom of Pawlett Hill, on its western side and close to the start of White House Road, is a gigantic, rusting, corrugated-iron, 'Dutch-barn.' It peers over the surrounding trees with mysterious intent, horizontal panels of dark glass high up along each side, its approaches guarded by mouldering notices to 'Keep Out.' It belongs to a 1950's TV episode of 'Quatermass.' I'm told this was once a barrage-balloon factory, in service during the last war. Lurking in such an 'out of the way' spot, you wonder what could be going on there now. There's not much of a call for barrage-balloons these days...

The barrage balloon building, Pawlett

The River Parrett arises amongst a multitude of springs north-west of the Dorsetshire village of Chedington; about 10 miles south-west of Yeovil. The newly born river then passes through the village of South Perrott and, in less than a mile, crosses the county border into Somerset. It then flows a mile or so west of North Perrott travelling on, virtually due north, through the county and it seems likely the river shares the origin of its name with the two Perrott villages close to its source. In Somerset, the Parrett passes through the Ham stone district between South Petherton and Martock, entering the Levels at Kingsbury Episcopi and Muchelney. A few miles south of Langport, the Parrett receives the tributary rivers Isle and Yeo and about here starts to experience the tidal effect of the Severn Sea, still 20 miles (32 km) away. It then turns from north to north-west passing below Burrow Mump at Burrowbridge where it is joined by the River Tone and on across the Levels, gathering water from innumerable rhynes, to Bridgwater.[32]

West Quay,
Bridgwater

[32] *The 'e' has come and gone from Bridg(e)water for ages, but its absence is now jealously guarded. The name seemingly arose from one of William the Conqueror's followers, Walter de Douai, taking over the area and the crossing - thus; 'The Bridge of Walter.' Almost too tidy to be true! You can understand why Walter lost his 'l' but it doesn't explain why the 'e' went missing. My Ordnance map of 1809 has the 'e' there in big writing. So maybe it was just a difficulty with spelling. Just to confuse things; the 'bridg' part may not have been a bridge at all but derived from the Norse 'bryggia', meaning a jetty!*

The Parrett, central to Bridgwater's existence, passes close to the centre of the town. From the Middle Ages, it became an important port and ship building centre. In 1841 a tidal basin and docks (a 'floating harbour') were constructed which also linked the river with the new Bridgwater to Taunton Canal. The really good times lasted just 20 years or so; with the expansion of the railways and the opening of the Severn Tunnel in 1885, river trade followed an inexorable decline. Few ships used the docks or the canal after the First World War and they were officially closed in 1971. Since the 1990s the area has been redeveloped; the docks becoming a marina and the grand Canal Company warehouse converted into flats, offices and a pub - 'The Admiral's Landing.' The canal too has been reclaimed and is open once again - though mainly for small boats and holiday barges. Some of the old commercial atmosphere remains, captured by the splendid Bowering Animal Feed building with its chequered stone and brick high-chimney, still busy in the western corner of the harbour. But the Parrett has always been an awkward cuss. While I was looking around there was not a yacht to be seen; it is virtually impossible for a boat to get out of the river and back again on a single tide, and this precludes the average yachtsman, who might want a few hours sailing with straightforward access to the sea.

Bowering's buildings, Bridgwater docks

During Victorian times and the early part of the 20th century, the banks of the river were lined with industry and the most important of these were the various brick and tile works.[33] They produced the superb warm terracotta brick that I describe in the chapter on Burnham. There must be buildings the world over still glowing with Bridgwater brick!

A heap of Bath Bricks

Many of the brickworks had their own wharfs, close to the clay pits and brick kilns. The clay pits are still there - great water holes alongside the course of the Parrett - from Dunwear to Dunball and Combwich.

Although the ships are gone, the centre of Bridgwater retains the atmosphere of a small port. Along West Quay, 18th and 19th century buildings press close to the river. There is a variety of gable heights and designs (some show a strong Dutch influence) which give the quayside a lively and individual character. This is reinforced by the substantial iron balustrades and railings which defend the town's citizens from the river and its 'algal slime'. Running up from West Quay are a series of beautiful streets, some elegant like the Georgian terraces of Castle Street, others medieval as in Dampiet Street where Samuel T. Coleridge came to preach at the Unitarian Chapel in 1797/98 and which still stands. Bridgwater's most famous son, Admiral Robert Blake, is remembered at the Blake Museum (in Blake Street!) which occupies his 15th century home.

[33]*One product of the Bridgwater brickworks was especially successful in its day - the curious 'Bath Brick.' Apparently the silt in the Bridgwater zone of the Parrett had a particular combination of sand, clay and algal slime (!) which, when baked and powdered, was used as a scouring agent. Too far down the river and the mud was too sandy, a short way up and there was too much clay. When fired, the bricks had a pale yellow colour vaguely similar to Bath stone - hence the name (though it has been said that they were invented by a Mr. Bath). Nowhere else in the world could (or tried to?) make Bath Bricks and for over a century Bridgwater was turning them out by the boat load - at the height, over 24 million a year! Production closed down in the late 1930s as more sophisticated cleaning agents arrived on the market. When you look at them today - in their glass case at the Blake Museum in Bridgwater - they look like ... well - bricks! How could anyone clean anything with a brick? And 24 million a year...*

The Bridgwater Carnival

The Bridgwater Carnival is a fantastic local tradition. These days it involves floats and displays illuminated by thousands of bulbs parading before a street audience of over 120,000! It's reckoned to be one of the largest and most spectacular night-time carnivals in the world.

Its origins do appear to centre around the celebration of Bonfire Night on November 5th and the 1605 failure of Roman Catholic Guy Fawkes to blow up Parliament was something that Protestant Bridgwater felt rather strongly about. In Bridgwater the bonfires came to be built around a worn-out boat loaded with tar barrels. Indeed there was a time, as Bonfire Night approached, that the supply of redundant boats ran out and perfectly good craft went missing from the harbour!

The night began with a procession past the unlit fire standing on the Cornhill in the town centre, which was then ignited by the vicar of St.Mary's Church - in later years he was assisted by paraffin and enthusiasts with burning tapers. The fire would explode into life, shooting flames high above the town.

Tarmacked roads put paid to the Cornhill bonfire in the mid-1920s, so the town folk's energy now flowed into the procession. Various pubs had previously competed in making Guy Fawkes effigies and parading them in horse-carts before they were hurled onto the fire. These 'gangs' now constructed amazing set-pieces either motionless (tableau) or moving (feature). With advances in technology these floats have become more and more extraordinary.

After the procession 'The Squibbers' come into play. These are over 100 brightly dressed individuals holding squib fireworks at head height on what amounts to a broom handle ('the cosh'). The squibs were originally home-made from rolled paper stuffed with gunpowder, with a touch of 'rock-powder' at the bottom for a final BLAM!!! A certain John Taylor succeeded in blowing up himself and his family, making squibs at home. Before 1881 the squibs were let off at any old time, day or night, with the associated risk of serious injury. These days it is a safer, but still spectacular, affair.

Although Bridgwater is the Grand Occasion, the carnival has now moved out to other Somerset towns - North Petherton, Burnham/Highbridge, Shepton Mallet, Midsomer Norton, Wells, Glastonbury and, with a great finale, at Weston-super-Mare.

The Parrett winds on through Bridgwater, with another 11 miles (18 km) of twisting and turning to do before it gets to the sea. The river is hugely tidal, an effect amplified by its horizontal progress across the Somerset Levels. On the incoming tide, ships could gain access to and from the Bridgwater docks quite easily, but they only had so much time. If time ran out, the boat would be stranded on the mud banks and, if loaded with bricks, could topple and capsize.[34]

Most people have heard of the 'Severn Bore' - the famous tidal wave formed by the funnelling effect of the Severn Estuary and the enormous tidal rise. Well, not surprisingly, the Parrett has a small Bore of its very own. Admittedly the wave doesn't usually get much higher than a foot or so, but under extraordinary conditions - spring tide/onshore wind/low air pressure - it can rise to several feet. In 1875 it rose to 10 ft (3 m) and flooded much of the Levels. Writer Brian Waters quotes an old woman's description of the twisted meanderings of the Parrett from Bridgwater to the sea, as being "as crooked as a barrow pig piddling in the snow..." And it does appear to have a singular lack of self control. The river makes a number of violent diversions and, like the road to Brean from Weston, often succeeds in travelling in the opposite direction to where it's going to end up.

Downstream from Bridgwater the Parrett slides by two final settlements. The first it encounters is Dunball Wharf which started life as a small hamlet to the village of Puriton. The M5 motorway put an end to that when it slammed its way between two communities already divided by a railway and a trunk road. But even worse for Puritan folk was that; "...it buried the lane where the first early violets were found."

[34]*In 1867 a 60 ton ketch 'Fame' fell over at her brickyard wharf
because her skipper hadn't tied her up correctly.
On that occasion it was possible to refloat her on the rising tide.
Some time later she grounded on the east bank
of the river. And that did for her. For over 100 years 'Fame's' timbers could be seen,
slowly rotting away, upstream from Dunball Wharf.*

Combwich Pill

By the river, Dunball Wharf[35] has held on to a fair amount of shipping trade with timber from Russia (which has replaced Welsh coal) and, rather closer to hand, gravel and sand dredged from the Bristol Channel. The proximity of motorway and railway have helped to secure its survival but the ships require skilled pilotage to make safe passage along the 10 miles (16 km) to and from the sea. At Dunball, the river turns between high banks of sand and mud, gradually widening through the Pawlett Hams in a huge 'S' bend to arrive at Combwich.

[35] *Dunball Wharf was constructed in 1844 by Bridgwater merchants to speed the transport of coal - they set up a horse powered tramway to link up with the Bristol and Exeter Railway. But the place goes further back; local legend has it that in medieval times there had been a landing close to Dunball, at Knowle Hill, for pilgrims on their journey to Glastonbury.*

The 'fives' wall at The Anchor

Combwich (pronounced 'Cummidge') looks curiously isolated on the map, as indeed it used to be before Hinkley Point Nuclear Power Station busied up the road. But Combwich Pill[36] had been a port since Roman times at least, and it is the obvious place - landing here avoids plying the precarious course of the river inland. Originally it might well have been the pre-eminent landing place with smaller boats taking on the transport of goods upriver. During the 19th century local farmers formed a co-operative called the Combwich Farmers Association which had its own fleet of boats. So did Henry Leigh who owned the local brick yard. Leigh built Tower House with its tiara-topped observation turret (still there) - all the better for watching the comings and goings on the river! Successful trade led to a period of real wealth in the community with merchants and sea-captains building houses around the Combwich creek.

[36] There is a fancy the village got its name from Dame Withycombe, the dreadful Witch of Combwich. It seems she polished off three husbands by pouring molten lead into their ears! Doesn't bear thinking about. Actually the name goes way back, Domesday gives it as 'Comich' or 'Commitz' and it's difficult to wheedle a witch out of that. A 'pill' is a term used almost solely in the Severn Estuary and Cornwall to describe a small tidal creek. OED.

According to historian Grahame Farr, the last trading boat of the old style entered Combwich Pill in 1949, but it didn't get anywhere - with lack of use the creek had silted up. During the construction of Hinkley Point Power Station in the late 1950s, the pill was substantially upgraded so that heavy equipment could be brought in by sea. More recently the power station jetty has been further improved to take the occasional 'Roll-on/Roll-off' ferry. Nowadays little commercial use is made of the creek itself and the silt is returning, but it is still used by the Parrett Boat Club. The power station maintains a laboratory on the wharf which keeps a regular environmental check on the area - land and sea. All clear so far!

Tower House,
Combwich

As I've described earlier (from the other side of the river), Combwich nestles at the edge of the Quantock Hills with the old village pleasingly arranged on gently rising ground. New building on its southern borders, as is usual now, makes little reference to local character. Combwich has two pubs with a nautical slant and both date from the late 17th century. The Old Ship sits back up the hill with glimpses of the Parrett at the bottom of the road.

The Anchor Inn, standing lower down, across the road from the grassy bank of the river, is…well…just a little odd.[37] It's as though a 1930s cruise liner has been grafted onto the front of a Somerset farmhouse - all blue and white, with horizontal railings, portholes and a funnel. The high deck looks across the village green[38] and the Parrett, towards Pawlett Hill. It's a fine setting for a Pimm's on a summer's evening. Next stop Montego Bay…

Wooden buoy, Combwich Pill

[37] *And just as mysterious is the old high brick wall on the north side of The Anchor's car-park. This turns out to be a Fives Court. Perhaps Henry Leigh just happened to have a surfeit of bricks one time, which he didn't know what to do with? And how come they were playing fives in Combwich?*

[38] *The village green used to accommodate the local cricket pitch. According to local historian Bill Johnson, a small cricket pavilion, donated by a certain Martin Felstead, arrived as a 'flat-pack' and was left unopened on the riverbank. It promptly floated away on the evening tide.*

As well as being a harbour, Combwich was the first crossing point providing access into north Somerset from the west. Glastonbury pilgrims certainly crossed here. At low tides it was even possible to ford the river on foot (along a ridge of Blue lias rock) and avoid paying the ferryman. The travellers would call at the White House Inn on the opposite bank to wash the mud from their legs and feet. And there are stories of children making their way across to pick blackberries and scrump apples from the trees in the garden of the same White House Inn. I don't fancy trying that today. Old Man Parrett rolls on four more muddy miles before it gets to the sea, passing, on its left bank, the strange land of Steart and its island.

The Gore buoy

Chapter Four

STEART

Reed beds on the Steart levels

Lying low, almost unseen, between the Parrett mouth and the rise of the Quantock Hills, hides the land of Steart.[39] In character it belongs to the Somerset Levels; drained marshland vulnerable to flood, but its proximity to the open sea imparts its own peculiar nature. On the map it looks like a ballet shoe, with the foot 'en pointe,' connected to the rest of Somerset by a short, plump ankle. Steart is gained by a solitary, narrow road (Stert Drove) threading 4 miles (6.5 km), north-east, from the villages Otterhampton and Stockland Bristol.[40] Along this thin road the skies are wide and open, the raised shingle sea-embankment fringed by reed beds and hummocked dunes and the grey, cuboid, fortress towers of Hinkley Point visible in the west across the Stert Flats. Also unsettling are the introverted sheds of several intensive chicken farms and the faint whiff of their ammoniacal litter.

[39]*Steart or Stert? The spelling wanders from one to the other. I have no idea why.*

[40]*Otterhampton has nothing to do with otters unfortunately. The otter bit probably came from a minor Saxon nobleman called Otrame. The oddly displaced Bristol part of Stockland is due to its connection with a 13th century hospital built in the city by a Maurice de Gaunt.*

Salmon, Elvers and Eels.

The eel and salmon, though unrelated species, have similar life histories in that they leave
their home river and freshwater environment to spend varying periods in the salt-water of the
Atlantic Ocean. The adult salmon returns to its river to breed whereas the eel does the opposite;
it leaves the river for the ocean (The Sargasso Sea) to reproduce. The larvae and then the young
eels (elvers) journey from the mid-Atlantic, guided by the 'smell' of fresh water,
to the rivers of Northern Europe.

With pollution and overfishing, the salmon has almost disappeared from the Severn Estuary but,
before the 1930s, the fish was still caught in fair numbers. In Bridgwater this was done by
dip-netting - the muddy waters of the Parrett would clog the salmon's gills bringing the fish close
to the surface where a net could be dipped under it. At the river mouth, funnel shaped baskets
('butts') were erected in 'weirs' and, as the sea ebbed, the salmon were trapped.
Both these methods of fishing, together with the 'flatner' boat; its small draught ideal
for the estuary's shallow waters, are now slipping into folk memory.

River-poison and exploitation have also struck the Common eel but, despite that, the silvery
juvenile 'glass-eels' - the elvers - still arrive at the Severn Sea in vast numbers.
They enter the Parrett in spring on a night flood tide, pressing on past Dunball and Bridgwater,
to Burrowbridge and up the River Tone. From all along the Parrett and its tributaries,
if they escape the close gauge fishing nets, the elvers move out into the rhynes and waterways
of the Levels. Here the eel feeds and grows for 8 years or more,
by which time it is ready for its 4000 mile (6,500 km) Sargasso return.

In October a big tide will push the salty smell into the marshes and rhynes. If it is dark and
stormy, "between the last and first quarters of the moon," the eels might emerge. Should they be
landlocked they will cross pasture and open grassland to gain the main watercourses,
driven by some primeval trigger towards the open sea. For hours the land and the rivers can be
alive with their snakey flickering and then, as strangely as it started, they will be gone.

Cox's Farm

Steart hamlet consists of a cluster of farms, gathered over its instep, set back a short distance from the marshy fringe of the seashore. The farmhouses are mostly small and whitewashed, set low, and sheltering behind ponds and lawns, their barns and boundary walls constructed of large pebbles held together by lashings of mortar which makes them look endearingly home-made. In a field, set back from the road at Church Farm, stands St. Andrew's Church[41] whose bright red brick seems a long way from Bridgwater. Manor Farm, the last house on Steart, stands alone somehow, with no trees, bleak to the wind, a gated track leading into the Bridgwater Bay reserve.

Little egret

[41]*During a night in June 1986 the church was struck by lightning. The bell tower caught fire and collapsed, the half-hundredweight bell crashing to the floor. The font, lectern and prayer books were rescued by villagers, but the altar was badly damaged. A crucifix and brass candlesticks melted in the heat.*

The other way to Steart is along the tractor lane from Combwich which doubles as the closing chapter of The River Parrett Trail. It starts just north of The Anchor Inn, below the raised river bank. When Rosie and I walked this way in January, it was sheltered from the cold north-west wind by high hedges of hawthorn and willow (leafless but still effective!), the occasional gorse bush was in full flower, but just putting your head above the bank introduced an uncomfortable degree of chill. The river slid silverly by, high pylons from Hinkley striding into the east. We crossed the fields to Steart, passing farmhouses which, like us, had their backs to the wind.

From River Parrett west bank, looking to Combwich

The toe of Steart ends at Stert Point which, combined with the curiously named area 'Fenning Island' (presumably because it once was), has become home to the Bridgwater Bay Nature Reserve. Many acres of mud flats reveal themselves at low tide, with the marshland and river silt, they allow rich feeding for wading birds like curlew, dunlin and redshank. On one occasion I saw a Little egret stalking the rhynes - bright white, heron-like, with a plumed head. The reserve has provided a dramatic wooden bird-watching tower (designed by Wilf Burton and Tony Eastman),[42] which as well as being ideal for observing all the ornithological activity is a conversation piece in itself!

---

[42]*I think it could be a distant galactic outpost for a character out of StarWars. But Rosie doesn't agree.*

The bird-watching tower,
Fenning Island, Steart

But it does seem strange. When you
reflect on all the defended wild life freely
arriving, freely departing, tucking-in
along the shoreline, while at the same
time, and just a few miles away,
others of their kind are living out
short, sequestered factory lives; all
for a place on a supermarket shelf.

Pebble wall, Steart

Warning
This is a
Farm Watch
patrolled
area

V R
POST OFFICE

From the bird-watching tower at low tide, you can watch the closing episode of the Parrett in its mud cloaked groove, as it gives up its waters to the Severn Sea. Joined by the Brue, it makes a right angled turn about Stert Island[43] and flows westward into the Channel.

[43]*Stert Island, for all its flatness, does manage to keep itself above water - just. Astonishingly on the 1809 Ordnance map there are a couple of cultivated fields and a dwelling called Warren House, which must have had a heck of a damp problem. But maybe they just bred rabbits. These days Burnham Yacht Club, depending on weather and tide, makes a summer evening landing on the island, enjoys a barbecue and then waits for the morning tide to carry them home. That seems to be far more sensible.*

Steart

Manor Farm   Stolford   Hinkley Point

8.15 am. Just off the Parrett mouth, close to the Stert Flats and Stolford.
The Quantock foothills rise up behind Stockland Bristol. We can just make out Minehead's North Hill in the haze.
High pebbled beach at Stolford. Glastonbury Tor! Andy catches sight of the Gore buoy. Sue at the helm.

Chapter Five

FROM STOLFORD TO HINKLEY

The Sellick mud-horse

The shoreline's slow curve from Steart to Stolford changes from tussocky dunes
and saltmarsh to a foreshore where the tide has formed a low pebbled embankment,
extending a hundred yards or more at low water. Beyond the pebbles lie the mud zones
of Stert Flats. On the landward side of this natural causeway is a wide, often wet, area
known as Catsford Common bounded by a grassy embankment defending the farmhouses
and cottages of Stolford. From the shore, Stolford sits well down and must be below
sea-level at high tide. The farms here are truly old and names like Stolford, Chalcott,
Whitewick and Zipe Farms occupy the same positions on my 1809 map (although 'Zipe'
was spelt 'Zine') as they do today. North of the causeway, opposite Stolford Farm,
at extreme low water on a spring tide, the remains of a submarine forest can be seen.[44]

[44]*Only 8,000 years ago it would have been possible to walk across dry land, to the islands Steep and Flat Holms.*
Post-glacial woodland slipped beneath the waves as the waters rose with the melting ice -
evidence of the varying sea levels in the Bristol Channel during relatively recent geological time.

Stolford Beach

Like much of the area between Burnham and Hinkley, Stolford was a rich fishing ground, but the 6000 mud-flat acres (2,400 hectares) of Stert presented a particular opportunity and challenge to the local fishermen. So they developed a device called a 'mud-horse,' a sort of mud toboggan, which allowed them to sledge over the flats (where the mud can be up to 6 ft/1.8 m deep) to their staked nets. At one time there were a good few men from Steart and Stolford who fished in such a way - as many as twelve within living memory. Today the number has shrunk to two: Brendan Sellick and his son Adrian.

One summer afternoon, about an hour before low water, Brendan took us out over the rocks and mud, a quarter of a mile from the shore. Adrian was already much further out, at stakes barely visible and up to his shoulders, with the tide still retreating. "He'll be up to his neck in it" said his father. The mud-horse was parked weighed down with stones, and we were shown how it could skid across the mud with a fair weight on board.

Sellick's Fresh Fish

It's not unusual to catch 50 lb. of fish and on a good day it can exceed 120 lb (55 kg). In winter they catch cod, whiting, plaice and sprats, and in summer they'll get sea-bass, skate, conger-eel, Dover sole and grey mullet - they also harvest the small sweet local shrimps. The Sellicks are still selling their catch from a small wet-fish shop next to their pebble walled home, 'Mud Horse Cottage,' a short way back up the lane from the shore. A retired mud-horse rests atop a wall close by. We bought a sea-bass which we baked with butter and a squeeze of lemon. "Sweet..." my father would have said "Sweet as a nut!"

Stogursey High Street

Stolford may have been the port to Stogursey;[45] a fair sized village set back, 120 ft (36m) above sea-level, 5 miles (8 km) from the coast. The road through the village makes a gentle cottage-lined curve down to its renowned church of St. Andrew, built in the main by the Norman occupier William de Falaise at the end of the 11th century.

[45] *The Somerset dialect did for the original name 'Stoke Courcy' which arose from the land owning De Courcy family who acquired the manorial rights through marriage. 'Stoke' stands for a stockaded settlement.*

Almost immediately he gave it to the Benedictine priory of Lonlay in Normandy.[46] From the outside, with its peeling limewashed walls and copper spire, it looks rather careworn. But inside it delivers a huge surprise. Entering through the main West Door and advancing up the nave, you arrive at the Norman heart of the building, the Chancel. Suddenly the church takes on a different quality and scale: broad powerful arches supported by short, strong, stone columns, light slanting in through the south and east windows across prone white, marble figures. All this is enhanced by a stone floor sloping dramatically upwards from the nave to the altar, with two wide flights of steps to the sanctuary's high altar below the east windows.[47] It all feels medieval and not quite English.

The chancel, St. Andrew's Church

St. Andrew's name is also attached to a well just off the High Street. The "two fine springs" still flow from pipes in a small enclosed courtyard behind a red sandstone archway in St. Andrew's Road. Neither has ever failed and although both provided excellent drinking water, the right-hand spring was reckoned to supply the softest water - the better for washing clothes.

---

[46] *Stogursey has been 'twinned' with Lonlay since 1986. In 1440 Henry VI gave St. Andrew's and its priory to Eton College.*

[47] *In 1939 excavations, arranged by Revd. Basil Tucker, revealed the chancel's unusual sloping floor. They also revealed a spring which a dowser showed to pass 6 feet below the nave and west door to the stream bordering the south side of the church, thus explaining a damp problem. The prone figures are of William and John de Verney. In 1442 John was charged by the Archbishop of Canterbury for shouting in English, during mass, in Stogursey Church.*

Back in the High Street and turning south, along a raised footpath from Castle Street, you come to the moated remains of Stogursey Castle. Built by the De Courcys in the early 13th century it was to be destroyed and refortified several times. Around 1216 it fell into the hands of a serious baddy, Fulke de Breauté. He robbed and plundered the land between Bridgwater and Quantoxhead, its remoteness allowing him to get away with it for some time. In the end the Chief Justice of the Realm raised an army against him, he was brought to book and his fastness burnt to the ground. The two towers of the gatehouse date back to before 1300 and the castle walls possibly 100 years earlier. The thatched cottage, constructed within the original gatehouse, goes back to 1600 and is now let by the Landmark Trust.

The road from Cannington to Hinkley Point opened up this 'lost' area of Somerset when the first phase of the nuclear power station was built in the late 1950s. Before that it had loitered north of the A39, unseen as travellers sped by, heading for the Quantocks, Exmoor and the West. It remains rich agricultural land, fertile and well watered. It supports pasture and a variety of crops including a highly regarded newcomer, Oatley Vineyard. (See special page)

Oatley Vineyard during the vendange

Oatley Vineyard

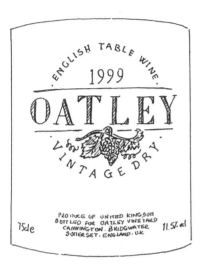

In the 1950s, camping in the Quantocks, I used to take a short cut off the A39, avoiding Cannington by cycling through Bradley Green and past The Malt Shovel Inn. Close to where I used to re-emerge onto the A39 there is a small deep lane (just east of Swang Farm) going down to Oatley Vineyard. The 17th century farmhouse occupies a fold in the Quantock foothills with fields sloping upwards to the east and west. In 1986 Iain and Jane Awty planted vines in the south-east field which had always been given over to the early peas. The vines are grown on simple vertical supports with the vine runners divided to grow along horizontal parallel wires.

The location suits the varieties Madeleine Angevine which produces an easy drinking 'Summer Dry' wine, and Kernling grape (a sport of the previously used Kerner, a Riesling cross, ripening some 2 weeks earlier than its parent) that makes the 'more serious' and prize winning 'Vintage Dry.' Both wines have a brisk, fruity, mineral acidity which makes them wonderful with food - especially fish from Stolford! The 'Vintage Dry' is long lived and continues to develop with keeping. Although the grapes originated in Germany, at Oatley they produce a wine with more of a French style, comparable to a good Chablis or Sauvignon. That's what I think anyway and I confess to gross bias.

In 1999 Rosie and I were invited to help pick the last of the vintage. The day before had been wet and dreary but, on the last day of October, we woke to clear skies and warm sunshine. The grapes were fully ripe, some grizzled and especially sweet. The harvesting took four to five hours and was followed by a fantastic meal in the lean-to barn supported by copious tastings from various years of the Vintage Dry.

A few years on from that October, I can confirm that the 1999 vintage, though small in quantity, is of high quality, crisp, steely and fruit-filled. It should develop for a good few years to come: folding the memory back, a delicious recollection of a golden autumn day.

Back at Stolford, to the west, the embankment rounds a low, blunt, promontory of large clattering pebbles protected by huge chunks of quarried stone. The stumped remains of wooden groynes stick up through the gums of the foreshore like decayed teeth, their defensive task superseded by the stony ramparts which extend from Stolford to Hinkley. Across the bay, Burnham makes a thin white line below Brent Knoll with Crook's Peak beyond. Brean Down and Sand Point then lead the eye to Steep Holm;[48] metamorphosed from its benign, currant-bun, Weston-super-Mare shape, into an island seemingly cliff-bound and inaccessible. As you round the Stolford promontory, the sombre citadel of Hinkley Point,[49] always on the edge of your vision, takes over the shoreline. It already seems to belong to a bygone age and a discarded technology. For all that, the reactor halls have a powerful presence, evoking the shore-forts of Northumberland.

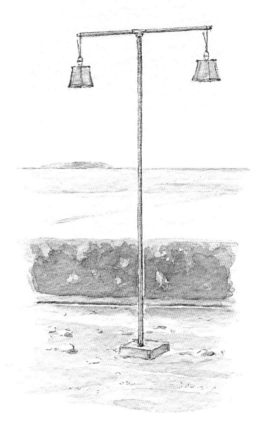

The 'tacky shades'

[48] *Steep Holm island has been described as "the full-stop to the Mendip Hills." It is a nature reserve, purchased in 1976 in memory of Kenneth Allsop, a pioneering environmental journalist. It's home to a great variety of seabirds, unique plants (eg. the Wild Peony), Victorian guns and their batteries, World War II remains (eg. searchlight posts), a restored Victorian Barracks and a ruined inn. And it's quite accessible - The Kenneth Allsop Trust sail weekly (weather and tide willing) from Weston-super-Mare, April to October. Information from the North Somerset tourist office. The island's story is wonderfully told in 'Steep Holm, the Story of a Small Island' by Stan and Joan Rendell, and also in a number of books by Rodney Legg.*

[49] *Hinkley Point scarcely exists on the old maps. On my 1809 edition it is shown as 'Inkley Point' (bar t'at?) - barely a point at all, more a muddy protuberance of the Stert Flats.*

[50] *The 'tacky shades' or mantles consist of a fine, sticky, gauze net which catches dust, debris, insects. From time to time the mantles are removed and analysed for radioactivity, pollution etc. at the laboratory in Combwich. Much of the testing consists of reducing the netting to ash which is then analysed.*

Behind defensive limestone boulders, the track towards Hinkley gives way to a concrete causeway which, while we were walking this way, accommodated a car and a line-fisherman or two. Walking westwards, the power station puts on cathedral clothes, towering behind high wire fences humming away to itself. Curious net 'lampshades' hung from outstretched arms on metal poles were placed at various points along the perimeter fence - we supposed that these were some kind of environmental check.[50] A walkway encircles the turbine halls and we were met by a kindly security-man who politely enquired what we were about.[51] Well, we were writing and painting a book...

Below the lichened walkway wall the shoreline began to take on a curious patterning. We were seeing clearly, for the first time, the limestone pavements for which, from Hinkley to Blue Anchor, the Somerset coast is renowned. There were succeeding stone ridges and steps which simulated the wave shapes of the ebbing tide, interspersed with pebbles and sand that looked to be lightly dusted with fine coal.

Out at sea, about half a mile offshore, the water inlet caisson for the power station generators stood like a sentry post to the mother fort, whose three great halls had retreated from view behind the high perimeter sea-wall.

Rosie's water brick

We turned the corner of the walkway and the high wall gave out to a flat open field - land that had been set aside for 'Hinkley C', a third nuclear plant which, for the present, appears unlikely to be built. The footpath returns to ambling and the shoreline begins to develop low cliffs above the pebbly foreshore. The cliffs reveal striking layers of different coloured rock; at the base, a blue-grey-yellow limestone known as the Blue Lias is followed by varying thicknesses of yellow siltstones and mudstones, grey sheets of crumbly shales and other bands of pale limestone. They tell stories of advancing and retreating seas, times when the waters were shallow and aeons when Somerset sank deep beneath the waves or rose high above them. The shore was strewn with bleached branches and tree stumps, Minehead's wooded hill just visible in the flat light of a March afternoon.

[51] *This was only a few months after the September 11th 2001 Twin Towers catastrophe in New York. So the polite enquiry was understandable.*

We cut south, inland and upward, along a sunken path with layered hedging on the western perimeter of the power station land. Clumps of daffodils bloomed against the blue backdrop of the most westerly station tower and sheep grazed in Hinkley C's field. The sign on the beach had directed us to the Wick Moor Drove - which is now the main road from Cannington to Hinkley - and we promptly got lost in the odd backland behind the station which claimed to be a 'nature trail'. We found the low barrow, known in these here parts as 'Pixies' Mound' and didn't surprise a single elf.[52] But it is strange to stand there, on top of something so ancient and to be fronted by the potent modernity of the power station towers. You can imagine, given a few more thousand years, two funeral barrows here: one memorial to the Bronze, and the other to the Nuclear Age.

Stolford, looking west to Hinkley

[52]*This is an Early Bronze Age burial mound, known to some as the Wick Barrow. When it was explored in the early 20th century a Roman coin was found inside - a practical joke by a Roman archaeologist? The mound has been the source of many 'fairy stories', peculiar noises and diminutive persons with red caps. One tale tells of a small, broken, bread shovel found on the mound being repaired by a kindly ploughman. He was rewarded the next day with a marvellous cake still warm from the pixie oven. Who would believe it!*

The Nuclear Power Stations at Hinkley Point

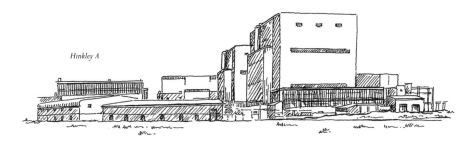

Hinkley A

The power station complex is an inescapable feature of the West Somerset coastline.

From Steep Holm to Burnham and Minehead its towers capture the eye,

the sun reflecting fiercely from its glass and metal.

The station represents two phases of nuclear reactor technology - Hinkley 'A' and Hinkley 'B'.

Hinkley 'A' occupied the two blue towers on the west side of the site. Work started on these in

1957 and required road improvements and a new dock at Combwich Pill. The station came

on-line in 1965. The blue towers (they were originally clear glass) housed two natural uranium,

carbon dioxide gas cooled, (Magnox) nuclear reactors. The reactors generated heat to six boilers

driving six turbo-generators which produced 430 megawatts of electricity.

They were permanently closed down in June 2000.

Construction of Hinkley 'B' began in 1967 and came on line in February 1976.

It is housed in the single huge alloy clad tower on the station's east side. It has two advanced

gas-cooled reactors using slightly enriched uranium dioxide. The reactors provide heat for twelve

boilers driving two turbo-alternators to generate 660 megawatts of electrical power.

Like a small offshore island on pillars, about half a mile out at sea, stands the water inlet caisson.

From here water is brought ashore (27 million litres an hour) along concrete tunnels to the

station condensers. When it's done its cooling work the water returns to the Bristol Channel

at an outlet about half a mile east of the intake. Occasionally conger-eels take up residence

in the system - they are usually discovered during cleaning -

achieving sizes of 20lb and more in the salubrious environment!

Continued

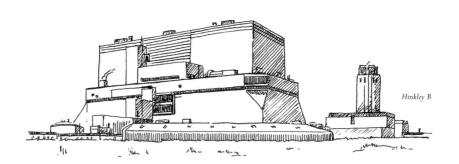

Hinkley B

When Rosie and I were escorted around Hinkley 'B' by Geoff Kay, we were hugely impressed by the attention to detail and cleanliness of the whole operation. The massive energy-roar in the turbine rooms seemed in extraordinary contrast to the quiet and the measured control of the nuclear reactor hall. Acknowledging all the dangers of nuclear waste, it was still a staggering demonstration of advanced technology. At its height the power station employed over 1,300 people.

The architect for the nuclear stations (A & B) was Frederick Gibberd who was also responsible for Stevenage New Town and the Catholic Cathedral in Liverpool. It is unarguable that the coastline would be better off without the power station, for this was a rare and precious environment before it arrived. But that said, both Rosie and I arrived at a reluctant fondness for the buildings, for there are times when the coast here can be misty and desolate, and Gibberd's halls, despite their modernity, lend a medieval potency to the scene.

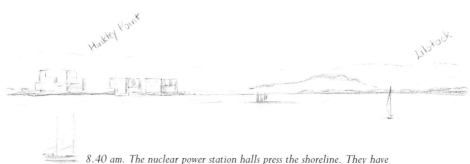

8.40 am. The nuclear power station halls press the shoreline. They have 'pac-man' faces. The water intake caisson looks to their bidding half a mile offshore.

Chapter Six

LILSTOCK AND KILTON

Lilstock Beach, looking east

From Hinkley Point the layered lias bluffs peel westwards to Lilstock;[53] the remnant of what was once a bustling Victorian harbour. By 1909, when writer Charles Harper dropped by, he was describing it as "...perhaps, not worth finding at all... a lonely cottage amid elms at the end of everything..." Well, it does take a little getting to and poor Charles Harper was distressed by a lack of signposts.

[53]*Lilstock is another place-name modified by the Somerset dialect. Originally it was 'Little Stoke'*
- a small stockaded settlement for cattle.

Getting to Lilstock is pretty straightforward these days: either along the coastal path from Hinkley, or the main north-west road out of Stogursey. Then it's up and down Cross Elms Hill, along the side of the valley facing Kilton, by-passing Lilstock hamlet, to arrive at a parking place tucked under a wooded coastal rise. A wide track, accompanied by streams on either side, leads up to the beach which is topped by a generous, grassy embankment running along the shoreline. Large lias pebbles are piled up on the seaward side but on the other is a wide stone lined gully; the inner harbour of the old port.[54] Originally there was a sluice gate which could be opened to scour the harbour and keep it clear.

At low tide the remains of the quay are still visible - huge blocks of stone, standing end-on, curve away into the water. Along the landward side of the inner harbour a row of cottages once stood, set into the hillside. There was an inn here too. Their storerooms, brick and stone archways, fireplaces and chimneys are still there, lost behind thickets of trees and bramble. Journalist Peter Hesp records talking to Mrs. W. Burge of Kilton - "I mind (sic) when there were ships coming in and out and Lilstock was a busy little place." The harbour was badly damaged in the Great Storm of 1900 and with a general decline in trade was never fully restored. A 1912 postcard shows the inner harbour in what seems to be good repair; a group of ladies are gathered

on the causeway, in the distance a car is parked in front of the cottages with another small crowd. They all seem to be having a really good time. A few years later the port's demise was probably settled by the First World War.

A day out at Lilstock harbour - from a 1912 postcard

[54]*The construction of the harbour was carried out by Sir Peregrine Acland of nearby Fairfield Hall (and St. Audrie's) in the mid-19th century. He used it to import and export coal, wheat and limestone. He lost his wife and four children to tuberculosis. Daughter Isabel was saved when he built a wooden house close to the shore, with a carriageway down to the quay. The sanatorium effect of this saved her life. In gratitude he constructed the splendid red-stone Gothic school in Stogursey. The school stands on 'Gallows Close' where two Stogursey men were hung, drawn and quartered following the Monmouth Rebellion in 1685.*

These days you may have Lilstock to yourself, save, perhaps, for a fisherman or two out on the limestone pavements. Hinkley Point power station arrests the eastern horizon and from here on the Somerset coast, it has an undeniable drama, somehow slotting into where your eye wants it to be. Below the causeway, the conjoined streams pour out onto the beach from a huge concrete pipe, the flow controlled by a formidable sluice gate. Along the embankment tamarisk trees indulge the west wind and the coastal path presses on, along the fragile cliff line. The crumbling lias has the appearance of earthy shale stitched together by an occasional band of yellow limestone, the sea munching away, remorselessly, below. Within a few fields the Royal Navy Range Quadrant Hut strikes a modern pose on the cliff edge. Looking out to sea you can make out the bright yellow target buoys demarcating the Lilstock Naval Bombing Range. If the 'hut' wears a red flag you may see some action!

Naval target buoys off Lilstock

St. Nicholas Church, Kilton

Lilstock hamlet, set back a little way from the sea, consists of a few farmhouses and the endearing, restored, medieval chapel of St. Andrew.[55] From Lilstock, the narrow road to Kilton recrosses the valley and then climbs up to St. Nicholas Church. Built of warm red stone with a small castellated tower, the church looks west to where the Lilstock valley gives out, beyond Kilton Wood, to the coast at Kilve and the glittering sea. The setting is perfection, but it must have been quite a walk to get to church.[57]

[55] *The chapel (all that's left of St. Andrew's Church, part demolished in 1881)*
came near to total destruction in the 1980s when it was 'declared redundant.'
It was saved by the energy and enthusiasm of Revd. Rex Hancock
who asked; "to lie in state there, before being buried."

[57] *When we passed by in March 2002, a notice lay in the church;*
'a declaration of redundancy on pastoral grounds.'

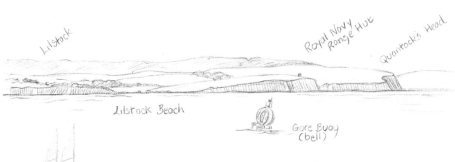

Lilstock

Royal Navy Range HUt

Quantock's Head

Lilstock Beach

Gore Buoy
(bell)

9.00 am. We can see Lilstock's wooded shore. Lias cliffs rise to Kilve.
A short distance away the rotund Gore buoy, bonneted in solar panels, dongs its bell. It leans in our direction,
the tidal current breaking around its base. Rosie's furiously sketching the shoreline.

Chapter Seven

One of my earliest memories of Kilve is arriving at the beach on a summer's day, to look for fossils. Instead of fossils I found a sixpence. Bright, silvery, shining up at me from between the pebbles. It seemed extraordinary amongst a billion grey pebbles, I should find a sixpence (a week's pocket-money in them days). And I never found another. But I have found quite a few ammonites.

A fossil at Kilve Beach

Having descended the long hill from Holford, there is still a sense of expectation as we turn off the A39. At first the road to the beach is rather cluttered with new building but the busy stream from Holford Glen still hurries along. There was a time when its progress would have slowed to do some work at the Kilve Mill. Nowadays it speeds straight on by, pausing a while at the pond at the bottom of Hilltop Lane.

Eventually the combe opens out at the whitewashed tower of St. Mary's Church looking out over the meadows towards East Quantoxhead. If you look inside you will see that the list of past incumbent vicars includes the name of Rex Hancock, who restored St.Andrew's chapel at Lilstock. A little further down the lane, you come to a collection of ecclesiastical ruins attached to a farmhouse. This is The Chantry[57] where you can 'bed and breakfast' or cream-tea beside the sheltering walls (no roof) of the old priest-house. I can recommend the coffee and walnut cake before sitting back to watch the sparrows noisily nesting in the chantry walls.

[57]*For many years called 'The Priory', although it never was.*
The buildings are 13-15th century and at one time five monks lived and prayed
here for the soul of their founder. The chantry proper was probably attached to the church.
Like so much of this remote coastline, Kilve was a smugglers' haven and there are
many tales of the old chantry being used to store contraband spirits. Up until the mid-1850s the
buildings were reasonably intact when a catastrophic fire virtually destroyed them.
It was local knowledge the combustion was much
assisted by all that high proof brandy!

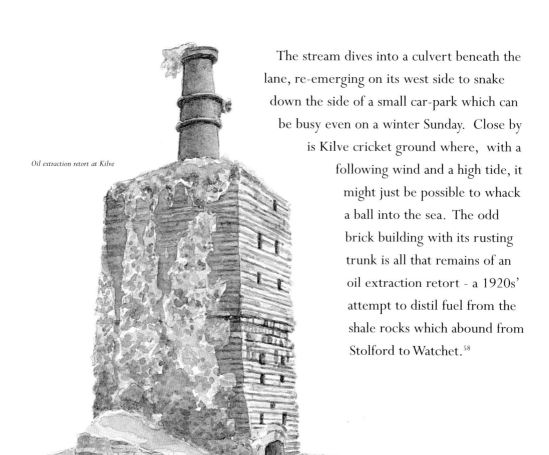

Oil extraction retort at Kilve

The stream dives into a culvert beneath the lane, re-emerging on its west side to snake down the side of a small car-park which can be busy even on a winter Sunday. Close by is Kilve cricket ground where, with a following wind and a high tide, it might just be possible to whack a ball into the sea. The odd brick building with its rusting trunk is all that remains of an oil extraction retort - a 1920s' attempt to distil fuel from the shale rocks which abound from Stolford to Watchet.[58]

[58]*In 1916 borings demonstrated oil-bearing shale beds to a depth of 1000 feet.*
Writer Berta Lawrence quotes with horror from the resulting investigation report:
"No mining is needed. The hills can be blasted down, great faces opened hundreds of feet high,
the rich oil-fuel picked up by steam shovels and loaded on rail trucks."
On top of that would have been the invaluable bonus of millions of tons of limestone.
Good grief. You can imagine the gleam in the oil-man's eye.
Fortunately by the late 1920s the gleam had dimmed
(high production costs), or the Quantocks and its coastline would have
ended up in extraction plants at Bridgwater. The retort is now a Grade 2
listed structure in an Area of Outstanding Natural Beauty!

Immediately beyond the retort lies a wooded area of boggy ground where the trees form a dark canopy. The Holford stream appears to have halted here, but the main flow continues on the western side of the wood where it has been joined by a brook running across the fields close to the church. The carcass of an old lime kiln lurks amongst the trees, mysterious, like the footings of an abandoned fort. A few more yards get you to the beach where the stream tumbles over the blue-grey pebbles. To the east a grassy slope[59] rises above the lias cliffs and on, past a small rampart perilously supporting a brick observation post. Westward, beyond the Quantock's Head escarpment, bights and bays lead to Minehead and Exmoor. Often there is a trail of steam left by the locomotive on the West Somerset Railway, chugging along the coastal track between Minehead and Watchet. Despite the railway, this place can be little changed from when the Wordsworths and Coleridge walked the shoreline (see the Special Page). The grey-blue sea still breaks over the limestone terraces which swirl away from the beach at low tide. The limestone is massive and smooth; great loaves of stone set close together as though by a master paviour. The whorl of a huge ammonite, up to 2 ft across, can fill part of the rock - this is what I was looking for when I found the sixpence - and Kilve is a favourite place for fossils (See Special Page 'Ammonites and the Blue Lias).

Kilve Beach

[59]*Called The Gallops because it was once used to train horses.*

On Kilve beach the great stone cobbles, set on their beds of shale, arc out from the shore.[60] It's sobering when you reflect that you are walking over the floors of ancient seas re-emerging, after 200 million years, through the erosive power of weather and tide. The cliff patterns at Kilve are rather different to Lilstock; they are 'younger' and contain a particular range of fossils. Going west along the beach, there are places where the blue-grey limestone ledges swoop up from the foreshore into the cliff-face, like the tilted platform of a cycle racing track. Occasionally the limestone strata have been eroded from within and spring water pours out from carious gaps in the rock. In several places the remains of old lime kilns are stranded half way up the cliff face, like fireplaces in a bombed-out building.

[60]*For many years Kilve beach continued to be home to the extraordinary sport of 'Glatting' - long after it had faded away in other places along the coast. Glatting was hunting for Conger-eels with dogs. The best time was in the autumn, when the spring tides are especially low. The fish are trapped in the rock pools as the sea retreats and the dogs smell them out. A good dog would take the conger in its teeth and eels up to 20lb could be hauled from its hole - dog and all.*

*Knapweed, cliff top
above Kilve Beach*

The sea's corrasion is slowly eating up
West Somerset. Some say that the original
village of Kilve stood on the cliffs looking
back to the church and was lost to the
tide's irresistible advance. I'm not so sure
our forefathers would have been so stupid.

The Delightful Shore

In July 1797 William Wordsworth and his sister Dorothy arrived at Alfoxton House near Holford. Their new-found friend Samuel Taylor Coleridge had been living with his family in nearby Nether Stowey since January, and it was Coleridge's entreaties that brought them to the Quantocks. The Wordsworths were able to stay for just one year. In that short time William and Samuel, with Dorothy's inspirational enthusiasm, laid the basis for the 19th century Romantic Movement which would revolutionise English poetry, opening the way for Keats, Shelley and Byron.

The three were great walkers, covering enormous distances and often setting forth on hikes lasting days, either together or alone. They explored the hills and combes, the dells with streams running through them down to the sea. They would climb to The Great Road above East Quantoxhead, descend Pardlestone Hill to Putsham (as 'upper' Kilve was then called), then on down, following the Holford stream to, as Wordsworth described it; "Kilve's delightful shore."

Once, unable to accompany his friends because of a scalded foot (his wife Sara had spilt boiling milk onto it), Coleridge, confined to his garden in Nether Stowey, imagines them walking through Holford Combe and up onto the Quantock ridge, the sun lowering over the Bristol Channel:

> *Now, my friends emerge*
> *Beneath the wide wide Heaven - and view again*
> *The many-steepled tract magnificent*
> *Of hilly fields and meadows, and the sea*
> *With some fair bark, perhaps, whose sails light up*
> *The slip of smooth clear blue betwixt two Isles*
> *Of purple shadow!*
>
> *(from 'This Lime-Tree Bower My Prison')*

The year together on the Quantock seaboard was intensely creative. From it sprang 'The Lyrical Ballads,' a joint collection, with poems like Coleridge's 'The Ancient Mariner' and Wordsworth's 'Tintern Abbey'. When the year ended, none of the friends would recapture the joy and happiness which was the source of some of England's most loved and enduring poetry.

Chapter Eight

THE QUANTOCKS AND HOLFORD

The Quantock ridge, looking to the Severn Sea, September

The Quantock Hills run back from the coast a distance of some 12 miles (19 km) occupying an area of around 50 square miles (12,950 hectares). The landscape is various and gentle: moorland of bracken and sweet scented heathers, wooded combes and glens with running streams, ancient mansion estates, red stone churches, a short spectacular coastline.

We used to camp by the stream in Holford Combe, my school-friends and I.
We pedalled heavy laden from Weston-super-Mare through Highbridge and Bridgwater
(complete with pong), on to the A39 Minehead road, through Nether Stowey to stop
for a rest by the old water fountain at the top of the hill on the outskirts of the village.
The road rolled on for a while until, turning off into Holford, we journeyed down into
the welcoming combe, a special delight that always felt 'just right.' It's much as I
remember; the open tree canopy with plenty of dappled sunlight in high summer and
open glades by the stream where it was comfortable to camp. I also remember a
cottage post-office on the narrow road that runs into the combe and a telephone box
where we able to phone home.[61] We would whizz down the long hill into Kilve to the
bakery there for crusty fresh bread. Not so whizzy going back though. These days I
pay more attention to the glorious view across the head of the Quantock Hills to St.
Audrie's Bay. The Kilve baker is long gone but the ammonites are still there in the
garden walls. Early one morning we were disturbed by the sound of horses crashing
through the undergrowth along the side of the combe. Poking our heads out of the tent,
someone called to us whether we had seen a deer. I don't think we were much help.

Holford Combe

[61]*Mind you, I was a little put out when my mum turned up early one evening
"Just to make sure everything's all right dear". These things are hard to live down.*

In the autumn my family would come to Holford Combe (Dad called
the village, stream and combe "Holford Glen") to pick whortleberries.[62]
I admit I was never too sure about whortleberries.
There was an awful lot of low picking with little
to show except stained fingers. And for me
whortleberry tart didn't come near Mum's red and
blackcurrant pie. But perhaps that was just prejudice
from too much low picking. They did look beautiful
though, those whortleberries, lying there, bloomy-black
in the biscuit tin.

Whortleberries

Holford is full of Coleridge and the Wordsworths. Alfoxton House,
where William and Dorothy stayed for a year in 1797-98, presents the same simple
classical facade to its sloping lawns. Glimpses of the house can be caught between the
trees as you ascend Longstone Hill from the Holford Green. Although the stream still
pours through the true Holford Glen close to the village, the waterfall is not the 'roaring
dell' it was in the poets' day. But, when the sunlight refracts in the fine spray and the
glossy hart's tongue ferns reflect what light there is in the ravine gloom, you're lost to the
romance of the place.

The atmosphere of the village is much as I remember it from my camping days;
the cottages that cluster around the entrance to the combe give way to the narrow lane
above Combe House Hotel[63] and end in the track through the wooded combe which
bears the village's name. If you walk up either Holford or Hodders Combes you'll
arrive on the Quantock ridge with the immense views across the Bristol Channel.

[62]*Whortleberry (Vaccinium myrtillus); also known as the Bilberry, Whinberry and Blaeberry in other parts of the
British Isles. Thrives on acid soils and in shade, which explains why it does well in the Quantocks.
As well as making a very nice tart, also once used in the preparation of a rich purple-blue dye,
which is why they're such good finger stainers! Closely related to the American Blueberry (Vac. angustifolium).*

[63]*The hotel was once a tannery; still functioning up to 1900. Its huge waterwheel was then put to the more
environmentally agreeable work of producing electricity. When Rosie was 16, she stayed here for a week on
a Local Studies course. "I visited a potter, walked to Alfoxton and learned to drink tea like a lady."*

Ammonites and the Blue Lias

Coroniceras lyra

From Lilstock to Watchet, the Somerset coastline reveals an extraordinary patterning and it's curious how bands of hard solid limestone can alternate with layers of soft shale. The dense limestones represent periods when the sea covered the land and the calcium remains of marine organisms accumulated and cemented together. The shales formed from mud deposits which were subsequently compressed. There is a whole range of shales, mudstones and marls which vary in composition due to the nature of their formation. Fossils in the denser limestones tend to be well-preseved - the harder rock is not so readily squashed. The order in which particular bands are laid down can be identified and the same sequences recur in varying positions along the coast. Earth movements and faults can bend and fracture the stratification but the order can usually still be distinguished (when you know what you're looking for!).

The Blue Lias ('lias' was a Somerset quarryman's term for 'layers'), a zone consisting mainly of bluish limestone and dark blue-grey shales, is the most striking geological feature of the West Somerset Coast. It also crops up in Lyme Regis, Dorset, and Whitby in Yorkshire, which, like West Somerset, are famous for their fossils. Along the Somerset coast the Blue Lias is at its most dramatic in the swirling, cobbled, beaches of Kilve and East Quantoxhead and it is the predominant member of what is known as 'The Lower Lias Group' in the geological strata.

Other zones such as the Doniford Shales and the Lilstock Formation (to mention a few!) have their own characteristics and fossils peculiar to the time and conditions they were being formed.

Ammonites, whose shells are such a fossiller's delight, lived between 417 and 65 million years ago (the Somerset cliffs span from 215 to 200 million years ago - the Upper Triassic and Lower Jurassic periods). It seems they departed with the dinosaurs. They belonged to the same class of animals as the present day octopuses, squids and nautiluses - the Cephalopods - and appear to be especially close to the Nautilus whose shell looks so much like the ammonite's.

Nautilus is a distinct order from the Ammonites - they have their own fossils - but they clearly shared many characteristics: a multi-tentacled animal occupying the large end-chamber of a shell which it's able to vary in buoyancy by either pumping gas (to rise) or liquid (to sink) into the smaller shell chambers. They move by water-jet propulsion. Today the nautiluses (who somehow managed to avoid becoming extinct) are found in the tropical Indian and Pacific Oceans, in deep water, on the sides of islands' submerged cliffs. Their shells are especially beautiful - coloured stripes on the outside and iridescent within.

The different geological strata tend to have unique ammonites. Indeed ammonites are one of the fossils used to identify rock age. Along the Somerset coastline, Kilve harbours the ammonites Coroniceras in its Kilve Shales and Metophioceras and Schlothemimia in the Blue Lias. Some of these can be huge and, thankfully, difficult to cart off the beach! At Doniford, specimens of the ammonite Psiloceras with its mother-of-pearl shell are fairly common - though I've never found one.

If you do go fossil hunting, remember not to be greedy. There certainly don't seem to be the ammonites just 'lying about' I remember a few years ago. Don't go tapping the cliffs with hammers - it's illegal. And keep away from the bottoms of the cliffs; a rock may fall on your head.

PS. In Somerset there is a legend that the ammonite fossils were snakes that had been turned to stone by St. Kenya - so ammonites were called 'St.Kenya's serpents.' In Whitby, the Abbess St. Hilda did the same trick when the town was infested by snakes. In both Somerset and Yorkshire the fossils often had a snake's head carved onto them. They were called 'snakestones' and sold as 'relics.' So, clearly, it was a fib worth perpetuating!

Bell and Common Heather

Rosie and I arrived on a sun-filled September day. It had been a wet summer and the heather had luxuriated in it. Now, the warm moorland was covered in a drift of soft purple heath and flashes of yellow gorse. The air smelt of honey. From where we stood on The Great Road,[64] the descending moorland folded into Smith's Combe with the pines on the knoll of Smith's Knap standing stagily to attention. Down the next combe, East Quantoxhead sneaked into view and beyond Quantock's Head, the Bristol Channel had on her very best 'smooth clear blue.' While we stood there, taking all this in, we became aware we had company; clusters of Land Rovers were pulled up along the ridge, their owners peering through field-glasses down into the combes. Suddenly, along The Great Road, a rider came in bright scarlet. Within moments, at a relaxed canter, he had disappeared over the hill-line and all eyes were fixed again on some distant activity deep in the combes. We had come upon the outer excursions of a deer hunt.

A rider came . . .

[64] *The Great Road, alluded to in Dorothy Wordsworth's 'Alfoxden Journal', is an old trackway from St. Audrie's and West Quantoxhead to Holford. It remains a grassy way across the head of the Quantocks with a multitude of combes running down the escarpment towards the sea.*

We continued on, down the Great Road and between the ancient Holford Beeches above Alfoxton. These trees may well have shaded the track the poets walked.[65] The beech is not a long-lived tree; 250 years is a good age and the Holford Beeches are beginning to look a touch senile. Great branches are broken from the main trunks revealing rotting heartwood. Saplings sprout from their composting interiors. Tree-man Alan Mitchell says an oak can take a century to die, but a beech will do it in a weekend. The Holford avenue should take more than a few days to return to the good earth, but their replacement can't be long off. So admire them now, while they are in their glorious and romantic decline.

[65] *These hills and combes remain a source of artistic inspiration.*
John Marsh's suite: 'The Quantocks, for violin and strings,' is a lyrical example.
Written as a tribute to Dr John Campbell it consists of four movements: Intrada - 'Arrival at Alfoxton,'
Nocturne - 'Holford Glen,' Intermezzo - 'Late summer days at Kilve,' Envoi - 'The road to Cothelstone.'

Chapter Nine

EAST QUANTOXHEAD

East Quantoxhead

Wall ammonite

From high on the Great Road, late summer and the moorland in a jazzy plumage of purple and gold. Before us Quantock's Head; the understated rise in the cliff headlands that marks where the Quantocks end and the Severn Sea begins. A field or two back from the shore stands the dark Court House, its church pressed tight behind it, both on a land-rise lifting them clear of their village, East Quantoxhead, to the south. From on-high this separation is not really apparent but, once in the village, the arrangement of the manor house, farm, its church and the limewashed cottages around the millpond is perfection. Arrival here is like coming upon a hidden secret: a community seemingly time-locked, enjoying a special serenity. There is a small car-park with a metal collecting box - so trusting and unassertive. It's all very reassuring.

A long limestone wall separates the grassy car-park from a collection of beautiful farm buildings with pantiled cowsheds and Hereford cattle. Incorporated in the wall are occasional large ammonites embossed with a gold crust of lichen. The path traces its way beside the wall and up a gentle slope. Through a small, inviting, gateway St. Mary's Church stands before the mullioned and tie-barred rear wall of the Court House.[66] Another gateway allows you to look back down the hill behind slate roofed and thatched barns, a manicured lawn leading the eye to a cluster of conical outbuildings against the green backdrop of East Wood.

On the east side of the millpond a path runs down behind the old mill house, passing by the beautiful Court House gardens. A stream runs on, its shallow banks covered with primroses in spring. From early March until late summer, the wet ground around the stream is almost choked with yellow-gold kingcups glowing in the damp shade. Looking back, the Court House stands sternly above a woodland garden. A house has probably been standing here since the 12th century but the present fortified medieval residence was largely rebuilt in the 17th century.[67] The pathway now opens out into a wide grassy track (which can get pretty boggy in wet weather) between fields, leading on towards the coast a few hundred yards away. To the east a footpath traces the seaward boundary of East Wood and makes its way across the fields to Kilve and St. Mary's small white tower.

[66] *The Court House is extraordinary for having been in the unbroken ownership of the Luttrell family for over 900 years - unique in Somerset. Various branches of the family occupied the house over the years and for two centuries it served as a farmhouse. In the 16th century a George Luttrell married out of his class to 'lowborn' Silvestra Capps - who hadn't learned good manners. Silvestra made everyone's life a misery, so George, in exasperation one day, threw her out of a bedroom window! Another story about Silvestra describes her doing the deed herself the next time; in a fit of pique, pitching her second husband, Edmund Skory, out of a window (George having shuffled off his mortal coil for a bit of peace). It seems people were flying all over the place. Anyway, Edmund then went and died and left Silvestra a prayer-book in his will and 20 shillings to his servant for having "lived under her tyranny". Unfortunately Silvestra got her revenge by outliving Edmund's son and a third husband into the bargain. Sometimes a bad mistake can end up lasting an awfully long time!*

[67] *Silvestra again. It seems it was her fault that "the whole place was turned back-to-front." Facing north must have made for a cold house with a fantastic view. These days, the prospect of the house from the cliff path, with a westering sun, is splendid.*

The seaward track arrives at the coast a short distance east of Quantock's Head. Here are steps down to the shore with a long-lost lime kiln abandoned at the top of the crumbling cliff face. On the beach below, the limestone pavements are lined up once again in fantastic formations - for this, like Kilve, is the Land of the Blue Lias. An easy climb westward brings you to the relaxed summit of Quantock's Head, some 60 ft above the sea. This is a good place to sit back with your sandwiches, face to the sun and back to the sea, looking across the fields to the Court House, the Quantocks rising to Longstone Hill above Smith's Combe.

The Court House from Quantock's Head

Continuing west, the high cliff suddenly dips down towards the shore while the footpath strikes inland along the field boundary. Half a mile brings you to small a burial-mound, about 8 ft high. When Rosie and I arrived, two pheasants took exception and took off with a clatter of wings. From the top of the mound we could see a pendant of small ponds running down a crease in the fields - at one time these may have supplied freshwater fish to The Court and the chantry at Kilve. Below us we could see 'Blue Ben' defining the western limit of the Quantock's Head shore - from thereon it becomes St. Audrie's Bay.

The Amazing Tale of Sarah Biffen

In 1784, a baby was born in one of the cottages that stand close to the stream that runs through East Quantoxhead. Sarah Biffen arrived in the world with no arms and no legs.

Against all odds, Sarah survived and developed a remarkable talent - by supporting a brush or pen from her shoulder, she was able to draw and write by manipulating it with her mouth. For a time she was exhibited in fairs and markets as a gifted freak, "a skilled painter of miniatures."

The Earl of Morton, suspecting skulduggery, invited Sarah to paint his portrait. At the end of each session he took the painting home so that no other artist could be involved. Assured of her honesty he became Sarah's patron and paid for her further training.

In 1824 Sarah married Stephen Wright at Kilton Church. He had plighted his troth in poetry:

> *"Sweet Biffen, though admired your charms,*
> *Your lover sighs not for your arms,*
> *He took the nobler part;*
> *And while your happiness he plann'd,*
> *Aware you could not give your hand,*
> *Aspired but to your heart."*

(And as things turned out, his affection was as shallow as his verse.)

For some time Sarah became celebrated and successful. She was honoured with a prize medal from the Society of Arts. She was patronised by royalty, including George III and Queen Victoria. But fame is a transitory thing. The Earl of Morton died and she was abandoned by her husband. Destitute, she was rescued by a Mr. Rathbone who took her from London to Liverpool and collected enough money to provide her with a small income. She died there in 1850.

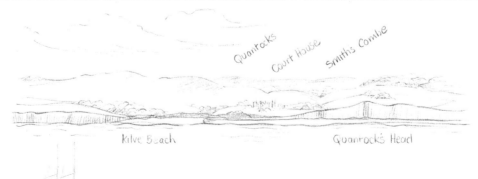

9.30 am. Kilve's layered cliffs dip and then rise again to Quantock's Head.
Through the glasses we can just pick out the whitewashed tower of Kilve's church peeking from behind the trees.
The dark Court House of East Quantoxhead is set against the purple-pink of the hills.

Westward shoreline from Quantock's Head

We made our way back, along a high hedged track decorated with a profusion of primroses, splashes of lesser celandines and greater stitchwort. Eventually this joined the road to East Quantoxhead, past Court Farm from where the stream could be seen making its way across the meadows towards the tower of St. Mary's Church and The Court.

Chapter Ten

WEST QUANTOXHEAD AND ST. AUDRIE'S BAY

Gatehouse, St. Audrie's Park

As the A39 swings round the wooded headlands of Stowborrow Hill, the land on its seaward side falls steeply away towards the coast. At the point where the road turns sharply south-west (before returning to its westerly course) a valley opens in a fold of the hillside. At the valley entrance stands St. Etheldreda's (St. Audrie's) Church, looking very spick and span,[68] a narrow private road passes by a small Gothic gatehouse

[68]*In 1909 Charles Harper described it as looking "astonishingly new." It still does!*

86

before travelling on towards the sea. In the distance, a manor house can be seen, with a tower and trees, surveying the Bristol Channel. It all appears very theatrical, because it is - the entire production was put together by Sir Peregrine Acland in the 1850s.[69] Sadly, as a result, West Quantoxhead lost its old heart and became separated from its school, church and manor house. The village, although wonderfully positioned, now has little shape and consists mainly of 20th century houses.

In 1934 the manor house and its grounds became a girls' school which survived for nearly 60 years. For a while it became a Buddhist retreat[70] before the house and grounds were recently reborn as St. Audrie's Park (complete with running deer) - an hotel that specialises in high class weddings. They were a little put out when they came across Rosie and I strolling down their drive. But quite nice when they discovered their "Private! No Admission. Definitely No Entrance" sign (next to the "Visitors this way" notice) had blown down in the wind.

Getting to St. Audrie's Bay is fairly straightforward. Although much of the land up to the shoreline is owned by two 'holiday villages,' public access is encouraged and has the advantage of some car parking. The 'villages' themselves are not overly intrusive as yet, although chalets and mobile homes are beginning to occupy higher land in the middle section of the bay. Both the camps belong to an earlier time - especially the one to the west, which still has some wooden chalets under trees and a deep stone clad gully down to the beach.

[69]*Cottages that interfered with the Grand Plan were removed and the main road bent south so it didn't mess with the vistas. The manor house was almost entirely rebuilt in a Victorian-Tudor style with a 4 storey castellated tower. The medieval church in the village was taken down and, in 1856, the new St Etheldreda was erected half a mile away, overlooking the estate. This Sir Peregrine Acland is the same man who built the harbour at Lilstock. His architect, John Norton, also designed St. Nicholas Church at Kilton and the school in Stogursey, which Sir Peregrine built to celebrate his daughter's return to health. Norton was the architect for the famous Gothic mansion at Tyntesfield, near Nailsea in north Somerset, now owned by the National Trust.*

[70]*Rosie and I met a chap who had lived there for four years during the Buddhist period. What he remembered most was the orangery - it had brilliant acoustics when he played his guitar!*

Blue Ben, St. Audrie's Bay

From the beach, the bay describes a wide shallow eastern bight with two deeper scoops to the west. The sand is reddy brown, with grey limestone pebbles, shelving gently into the sea. To the east, the cliff colour changes abruptly with the promontory Blue Ben where the Blue Lias strata give way to the Red marls of the Mercia Mudstones.[71] This area from Quantock's Head to Blue Anchor is riven with complex geological faults and folds.

[71] *The Mercia Mudstone group are the oldest rocks revealed along this part of the Somerset coast. They consist mainly of red-brown mudstones, with bands of grey and green siltstones (the Blue Anchor Formation) higher up. They formed within inland lakes which, in a hot, dry climate, dried out from time to time. They are virtually fossil free. The Mercia Mudstones occupy the Upper Triassic period - about 215 million years old.*

West of Blue Ben, the cliff-line softens for a while with grasses and bramble. A short distance from the promontory a grassy pathway, called Esson's Gully, slopes up from the beach.   From here the coastline loops away to Watchet, the shore a soft terracotta, the sea blue-grey, distant purple cliffs at first tree-topped giving way to open grass headlands. In several places streams break through the rock face. At Perry Gully the water cascades twenty feet in a series of angled falls, spilling onto the beach in an elegant arc. Nearby, the way from the holiday village follows a narrow zigzag path which, as we descended, felt rather like the start of an Enid Blyton 'Five Find-outers and Dog' adventure.[72]

Waterfall at Perry Gully

[72]*"Do you know," said Pip, "this is the fourth week of the summer holidays - the fourth week, mind - and we haven't even heard of a mystery!" "Haven't even smelt one," agreed Fatty. "Gosh this sun is hot......"*

The Acland dovecote

The western village is quite different. Turning abruptly from the main road, you follow a wooded track to a small parking place under the trees. There are some fine outbuildings of the old Acland estate here, including an octagonal dovecote (complete with white doves). The estate even had its own gasworks! From here, the way to the beach is down a deep spiral roadway with walls, like much of the estate, built of beautifully fashioned Old Red Sandstone, presumably from the quarries in Vinny Combe.[73] The road ends abruptly at some concrete steps. The red cliffs, which stand high and sheer from the beach, are partially faced with stonework that's being unpicked and undermined by the indefatigable tides. It looks as though it might slowly slide onto the beach, in a complete sheet of stone, at any moment.

Embedded in the sand are iron and concrete remnants of a jetty or breakwater, the ragged remains of the harbour the Aclands constructed to service the needs of their estate.[74] Up above, a stream pitches itself into space from the cliff top, landing with a vaporised crash onto the red rocks below. It's interesting here how geological forces have 'bent' the strata so the stone pavements are at right angles to the shore. The western promontory looks a mirror image of Blue Ben as the cliffs resume the stratified limestones and blue shales of the Lower Lias.

[73]*There is a clearly defined path up from the port, passing close by St. Audrie's House. It seems certain this was another Acland project and, like Lilstock, enabled the easy import of coal and the export of limestone and lime. It's probable the quarries in Vinny Combe, West Quantoxhead, used the harbour as well.*

[74]*Vinny Combe Quarry is set back in the headlands above the manor house. The track through the combe is one end of The Great Road from Holford. These days it is almost overwhelmed by rhododendrons (Rhod. ponticum) which are proving so difficult to keep under reasonable control.*

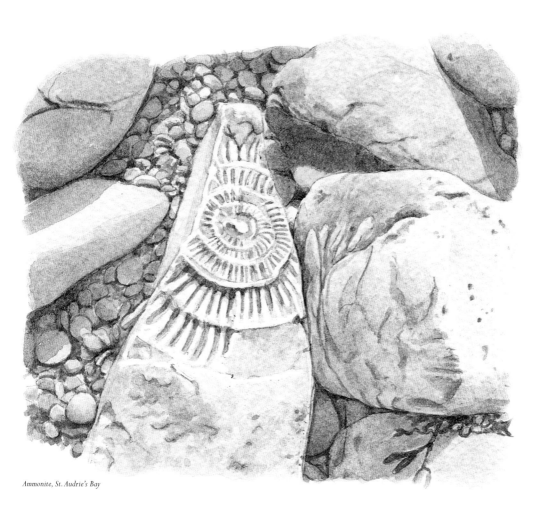

Ammonite, St. Audrie's Bay

9.45 am. The cliff colour flicks from grey to red and back again. From the boat, the promontory Blue Ben stands out in a bright grey-blue before switching to the mudstone cliffs of St. Audrie's Bay. Mobile homes gather at the cliff edge. The wind and the current are moving us along swiftly.

Chapter Eleven

DONIFORD BAY TO WATCHET

*Rosie's double
devil's toenail*

A round the western promontory of St. Audrie's Bay lies its rather untidy sister, Doniford. Just west of Doniford hamlet, a little way before the main road bridges the West Somerset Railway line, there is a short track leading to a small car-park with steps down to the shore. The shoreline is defended by grassy bluffs and outcrops of decaying red mudstone. The bay extends for about half a mile, along which the rocky layers present something of a shuffled pack. Limestone pavements, very similar to Kilve and East Quantoxhead are lined up along the shore. As before, these beds are rich in fossils and can contain huge ammonites (Paracoroniceras) nearly 2 ft in diameter. Doniford is well known for the much smaller Caloceras ammonite, jewel-like in its intact mother-of-pearl shell. It's alleged to 'frequently occur,' but I've never found one.[75]

Further out, towards the low-water mark, are sandstone beds which show the ripple marks formed as the land sank and the sea advanced. In some areas geological action has been so powerful the strata are turned on end and emerge from the beach vertically! The west cliffs are extraordinarily contorted with amazing twists and turns in the strata, made all the more remarkable by their bright reds, greens and greys.

The low cliffs of Doniford Bay were once home to anti-aircraft gun training. It started innocently enough as an Army Training Camp and was benignly welcomed by Watchet Council in 1925.[76]

---

[75]*Rosie found a double 'Devil's Toenail' (a fossilised bivalve shell - Gryphaea) on Doniford Beach. It lived for a while on our kitchen window-sill but then vanished. We looked everywhere. 'The Mystery of the Missing Double Devil's Toenail' - just the job for the Five Find-outers and Dog.*

[76]*The Army promptly restricted access to the foreshore with the result that the age-old Watchet small-fishing industry died.*

By the early 1930s the sound of gunfire and low flying planes was so deafening that the whole community was up in arms. Even the night hours were shattered by searchlights and high flying aircraft. Chunks of shrapnel fell about the place with quite a few close calls. All pleas failed. In the end (1960!) the Army was defeated by the sea eroding the cliffs and undermining the gun bases.[77] They agreed to a strategic withdrawal.

The West Somerset Railway makes its coastal appearance at Doniford, passing close to the cliffs at the western end of the bay before it curves 90° into Watchet above the harbour. Meanwhile, the sea is busying away.

'The Red Abbot,' Helwell Bay

At the Watchet end of Doniford Bay there's a smaller scoop out of the cliffs called Helwell Bay. Here the stone is soft and a rich red brown and huge fragments of the rock face have come away, leaving dark gaping wounds in the cliff face. You can see why the Army had to abandon their guns.

[77] *The hulks of the gun bases now litter the Doniford shoreline - massive circular concrete structures that have slid down the eroded cliff-face and lie about like abandoned millstones. Mysterious latter-day fossils.*

From the beach, Helwell Bay ends at a weathered cone of rusty mudstone; it looks like a great Red Abbot attending the approaches to Watchet harbour.[78] For Rosie, he sets off the scarlet lighthouse on the West Pier very nicely within the frame; the Indian red cliffs and the cerulean indigo sea... Beyond the Abbot, the scalloped edge of the cliffs runs out at the port's East Pier and its defending boulders of Mendip limestone.

The Washford River that runs through Watchet, begins its journey back in the Brendon Hills above Treborough. Following a twisted course, it flows down Druid's Combe to Roadwater. For a while, the small river accompanies Cleeve Abbey in its ruined idyll near Washford and then on, a further 4 miles (6.5 km), to Watchet. In Watchet, it has carved a substantial gully through the town and concludes its tortuous course, with a final right angle close to the Star Inn. It then dives below Market Street and out into the Severn Sea, west of the West Pier.

Goldenmean 'goosewinging'

[78] *The name 'watchet' is given to a particular shade of the colour blue or a cloth of that colour, traditionally a light sky-blue. Local historian Ben Norman speculates that Watchet cloth was dyed with whortleberries, but I'm uncertain whether that would impart what is understood as 'watchet blue,' since 'woad' was the universal blue dye. Which came first, the town or the colour? Also, was the Blue Lias rock a factor? In 917 its Celtic name was 'Waeced' meaning 'below the wood' (Robin Bush). King Charles I walked to the scaffold in a waistcoat of 'blue watchet.'*

Looking eastward from Watchet harbour

The mouth of the Washford River is, of course, why Watchet came to be. The bridge and culvert now make it impossible, but there was a time small craft could have travelled a fair distance inland on a high tide.[79] Today, boats arrive at a beautiful harbour protected by the substantial arms of the West and East Piers. From the sea, the West Pier lighthouse[80] is easily seen and welcoming. (The harbour has had quite a stormy history which is described in a Special Page.) In July 2001 a new Marina was completed which holds the sea within part of the harbour and allows boats to remain floating upright - rather than tipped over on the mud. Altogether more comfortable. It has brought a different atmosphere to the port, now tilted towards leisure rather than industry, something many locals are unhappy about.

[79] *The inlet was probably protected by a small breakwater and by the 13th century a quay had been erected. Before the early 1800s, when a stone bridge was built, the river opened straight onto the beach with a ford for Market Street. The river mouth was covered and culverted by the Mineral Yard in 1855.*

[80] *The cast-iron, hexagonal, tower was constructed in 1862 by Hennet, Spink & Else of Bridgwater for £75. The oil lantern top came from Stevens & Sons of London and cost £90. It was nearly lost after the 1900 gales, but not to storm damage. It had to be bought back from the demolition firm that had carted it off with the smashed Western Breakwater.*

'Ye Peere and Harbour of Watchplotte'

In the beginning boats simply moored in the mouth of the Washford River. Ben Norman has speculated that the small tidal basin on the south side of Market Street could be the inner part of the original harbour - no longer apparent since the river has been bridged and culverted.

By the 13th century a quay had been erected but was constantly buffeted by storms (one church raised 22 shillings "for ye repaire of ye Peere and harbour of Watchplotte"). By 1708 the old harbour was in a parlous state and Sir William Wyndham was authorised, by an Act of Parliament, to construct a new one.

The new harbour consisted of a single, western, semicircular arm (rather like Minehead today), 550 ft (167 m) long and built of "ruff stone - the best and largest that can be gotten in or about Watchet." By 1720 large cracks were appearing and, soon after, the quay-head had to be taken down and rebuilt with an extension of 50 ft (15 m). In 1797 a report from the great engineer William Jessop advised the construction of a stone East Pier. It didn't happen and, in the end, a much cheaper compromise of 'a row of piles braced from the inside' was erected and, as it turned out, gave little protection. In 1812 William's son, Josias Jessop, proposed an inner 'floating' harbour but this also came to nothing.

In October 1859 a violent storm raged all over Britain. Watchet harbour was severely damaged with 4 ships completely wrecked and one lost with all hands. The pier was breached for 20 yards (18 m). There were 3 plans for restoration (one by I.K. Brunel shortly before his death) and the smallest, cheapest option taken up. The West Pier was given a wooden breakwater extension of 390 ft (119 m) with a new East Pier, 590 ft (179 m) long, built of wood and stone. Within a year or so, the East Pier was beginning to crack. In December 1900, with high winds and

huge seas running in the Channel, the West breakwater and the East Pier gave way, exposing the sheltering ships to the full onslaught of the storm. Sea captains watched helplessly as their craft crashed against one another. 10 out of 13 were smashed and many of those boats were locally owned. The wreckage raised a mere £200 at auction. 3 years later, with repairs not yet complete, a further storm destroyed months of work and badly damaged a further 2 ships.
This time the West Pier was rebuilt of stone and huge concrete blocks, but the East Pier was, once again, restored as a wooden structure.

In 1935 the East Pier was, at last, constructed in concrete, but a warning that the West Pier also needed extensive repairs was ignored. 2 years later a gigantic fissure appeared along almost its entire length - 20 ft deep and 18ins.wide (6 x 0.5 m). An unfortunate dog managed to fall into the crack and had to be pulled out with a rope looped around a back leg!

Since forever, the local economy would rise and fall with the harbour trade, but that is a separate story. In 1993 the last local shipping company went into liquidation and the harbour was left 'redundant'. A Watchet and Somerset partnership was formed which, heroically, raised £3 million, from Government, EU and other sources, for a Marina Project. After much local anguish and debate, a Harbour Revision Order effectively closed the port to commercial shipping in July 2000 with the construction of the enclosing marina wall beginning soon after.
Watchet Marina welcomed its first boats in July 2001.

[For the full story read W.H.(Ben) Norman's 'Tales of Watchet Harbour']

There are times when Watchet can appear like a 1930's Railway Poster: the harbour sparkling in the sun, the boats bobbing, the sweep of the West Pier and its perfectly placed lighthouse, red cliffs and green hills, a steam train complete with steam, chuffing across the scene... The Esplanade, occupying the south-west area of the harbour, is wide enough to escape the shadows of the buildings that press up against it. The Coastguard cottages look very smart in their livery of white and blue, grey slates setting off the Red Ensign perfectly. The only thing that jars is the concrete pavier surface; it belongs more to a suburban shopping precinct than a harbour-side.

Swain Street

The Esplanade becomes Market Street at the point where the slipway runs up from the inner harbour and Swain Street strikes south through the town. On the Swain Street corner is the colourful 'Watchet Fruit and Veg.' - a shop that sells anything from bird cages and fishing bait to bookings for deep sea fishing on 'Seafire II.' Flowers and vegetables spill out onto the pavement as though there isn't enough room for them inside. The shop creates a marvellous market atmosphere in just the right place. Across the road, tight up against the opposing houses, stands the Watchet Market House, most of which is given over to a small intriguing museum - they've even got some mother-of-pearl ammonites. The local lockup[81] is located at the other end of the building and up some steps to the first floor is the tiny Holy Cross Chapel. For many years the Old Market House was a hardware shop with its arched windows and doorway opening onto Market Street.

[81] *This was the town gaol where miscreants who might "do a runner" were confined while awaiting trial.*
For centuries, the 'Watchet Court Leet' was responsible for the administration of law and order in the town.
The court sessions were held at The Bell Inn which still stands in Market Street close by.

Figurehead, Watchet Museum

Watchet Harbour's violent storms not only wrecked ships and breakwaters; they washed away many quayside inns and drinking-houses. Despite that, a good few of the present day pubs go way back. The oldest is probably 'The Bell' whose name crops up in 1744 and may well be 'The Three Mariners,' an ancient hostelry. 'The Anchor' was there in 1800 with 'The London' and 'The Star' soon after. Much of Swain Street is 19th century - rebuilt during the prosperous years when the Mineral Line[82] brought iron ore from the Brendon Hills. Houses on the Esplanade appear to be from the 18th century and there are cottages in Mill Street of 17th century origin.

Through the archway on Market Street and past the mysterious doorway to 'Sammy Hake's Cottage'[83] you come to the rear of The London Inn where the Mineral Line train once arrived. This area is still called the Mineral Yard. From here the tipping wagons moved along the West Pier and unloaded their ore down chutes into waiting ships. A few paces further westwards along Market Street, an entrance to a slipway takes you down to the small beach beyond the West Pier. The Washford River ends its journey here, rather despondently I feel, through a hole in the sea-wall.

---

[82] *Iron ore had been intermittently mined in the Brendon Hills since Elizabethan times. In 1853 Ebbw Vale Ironworks decided to exploit this resource by building the West Somerset Mineral Line to carry ore from mines at Raleigh's Cross to Watchet's West Pier, from where it was shipped to Newport. The line included an extraordinary three-quarter mile, 1 in 4, incline where trains were pulled up by cable winches. By 1898 cheaper Spanish ore closed the mines. An attempt to reopen in 1907 failed. The route of the line can still be traced.*

[83] *Sammy Hake was a fisherman / sailor who lived with his pipe-smoking mother in the cottage from the 1890s. Ben Norman tells me the door also provided access to the adjoining cottage by a passageway which also accommodated Sam's lavatory. Apparently the neighbours would often come upon Sammy sitting unconcernedly on the loo, greeting them cheerily as they passed by.*

Taking in the view

The last cottage on the seaward side of Market Street, immediately before the main entrance to the Mineral Yard belonged to a special Watchet sailor: John Short, known locally as 'Yankee Jack.' He sailed the Seven Seas, returning to his home port in the late 1800s. He had a beautiful singing voice and a phenomenal repertoire of songs and sea shanties.[84]

The view

[84]*His songs were collected by Cecil Sharpe and Richard Terry; both of whom were in some awe of his voice and memory. It is through them and John Short that we still have songs like 'Shenondoa' and 'A rovin' but, sadly, there is no recording of his voice. John died in 1933 aged 94 and singing to the end. He had the distinction of an obituary in The Times.*

I can't leave Watchet without mentioning its parish church, high on a hill above the south-western outskirts of the town. Much of the valley, between the church and the town, is filled by a paper mill[85] which once depended on the ships that used the port. St. Decuman's[86] is built in the Somerset Perpendicular style on ground that falls away sharply into the valley. Its fine tower is in curious competition with a handsome redbrick factory chimney close by. It's reckoned that St. Decuman's Church was the rendezvous of the three wedding guests, one of whom is "stopp'st" by Coleridge's Ancient Mariner, who then tells his dreadful tale. Legend has it that Coleridge and Wordsworth, on one of their famous perambulations, stayed at The Bell and wrote the opening stanzas of the great ballad. Watchet was the harbour from which the ill-fated ship set sail:

> "The ship was cheered, the harbour cleared,
> Merrily did we drop
> Below the kirk, below the hill,
> Below the lighthouse top."

A bronze statue of the Mariner (sculptor: Alan Herriot) now inhabits the harbour.

[85] Paper making has been a significant industry in the Watchet area since the Middle Ages. Esparto grass (for high quality paper) from Africa and wood pulp from Scandinavia arrived at the port, followed by a short rail journey to the factory. There was a time when dyes from the paper-works would change the colour of the Washford River; sometimes it might be green or blue, at others an unhealthy red! Much of the paper work now involves recycling.

[86] St. Decuman arrived in Somerset, from Wales, in the late 7th century. He had travelled on an improvised raft complete with a cow but, despite this, failed to impress the local inhabitants who chopped off his head. Undeterred, Decuman picked up his head, rinsed it in a nearby spring and plonked it back where it belonged. This clearly did impress the locals who converted to Christianity on the spot. His spring can be found on the side of the valley below his church.

10.10 am. Watchet's welcoming red harbour light waits at the end of the west pier.
Goldenmean is about a mile from the shore, and the small port appears contained within the natural rise of the hill
surmounted by St. Decuman's Church. Close to the harbour there is a blast of smoke and steam from
a locomotive in Watchet station.

The Two Rivers Paper Company at Pitt Mill

A diminutive tributary of the Washford River flows down a combe above Roadwater, arising close by Comberow and the famed 'Incline' of the Old Mineral Line. On its course it pours through the waterwheel at Pitt Mill and so drives the press of the Two Rivers Paper Company. Here, Jim Patterson the proprietor and Neil Hopkins his papermaker, work in the extremely wet craft of handmade rag papers with infectious enthusiasm.

Old cotton rags are macerated into a thin gruel and then scooped, with great skill, into a meshed frame where the fibres consolidate. The partially formed paper (it's a bit like sodden blotting paper at this stage) is then released from the frame, at just the right moment, onto felt rectangles that absorb the excess water, stacked, placed in the press and squeezed. After drying, the beautiful, textured, papers are ready to receive the watercolours for which they are designed.

Chapter Twelve

WILLITON, WASHFORD, OLD CLEEVE AND BLUE ANCHOR

The parish church of St. Decuman once presided over both Watchet and Williton and stood apart from both. Nowadays, Williton has grown into a small town, the seat of the West Somerset District Council, but it suffers the tribulations of having the busy A39 run through its heart. As you enter the town from the east, you pass an imposing sandstone building which would seem more suited to lording it over a manorial estate. This is the former Williton Poor Law Union Workhouse[87] built in 1837 for £6000. At the time of writing, it is being converted, with inescapable irony, into expensive apartments. The Williton district's particular claim to fame is that in 1170 it was home to two of the four murderer-knights of Thomas à Becket.[88]

[87]*In its workhouse days it could accommodate up to 300 sick and destitute people. These would include so-called 'imbeciles' who might spend their entire lives there. Inmates were employed in various soulless tasks such as "cracking stone for road-making." In 1948 it became an NHS hospital for the elderly infirm until it closed in 1989.*

[88]*Reginald FitzUrse lived at Orchard Wyndham and Simon de Brett at Sampford Brett. They both did penance for their crime at St. Decuman's church and Wells Cathedral. FitzUrse's heirs built a chapel at Worspring (now Woodspring, near Weston-super-Mare) dedicated to "the blessed martyr Thomas."*

A few miles along the A39, the road bridges the Washford River and turning, almost immediately, south to Roadwater you quickly arrive at Cleeve Abbey.[89] Even now, with Washford pressing upon its boundaries, it occupies a perfect pastoral scene. But when you come closer it exudes an atmosphere of destruction and loss, still present 450 years after The Dissolution of the Monasteries.[90] The mood is intensified because so much of the original building

The Gatehouse at Cleeve Abbey

remains; the cold dormitory where the monks slept; the extraordinary upper floor refectory with its carved roof and wooden angels gazing benignly on the action below; the low vaulted ceiling of the chapter house; the sadness of the absent church.

[89]*When Charles Harper passed this way in 1909, he had a run-in with the housekeeper - "an angry woman with inflamed visage and furious words"- upset because he had left his bike leaning against the Gatehouse and it was Sunday! No such problems these days; we were greeted by Maureen Freegard who, with her sister Dawn Berry (and before them, their father Sherbert Stevens), are very welcoming custodians with benign visages. The Abbey is now cared for by English Heritage.*

[90]*At the time of the Dissolution local gentry pleaded for the Abbey to be spared; because its priests were "of honest life who keep great hospitality." To no avail: the abbot and monks were pensioned off and, within a few years, the church razed.*

The Refectory with John Leach's pots

Back on the A39 and proceeding west from Washford, the return to the coast is best taken over the hill and through Old Cleeve.[91] This is a beautiful, compact, little village, gathered in the crook of the hill, to one side of and below its lovely church and enclosing an old orchard on lowering ground.[92] St. Andrew's backs onto ploughed fields, with its Perpendicular rusty sandstone tower looking out over pastures falling away to Blue Anchor Bay, Dunster's Conygar Tower rising from the plain in the mistful west. On a bright March day, high up at the back of the churchyard, Rosie and I gratefully looked out from a seat placed in memory of Angela (1957-1992) and had all of this to ourselves.

Westward from St. Andrew's Church, Old Cleeve, early April

From St. Andrew's with its Church Room close by the lychgate, the road tips past a cluster of thatched cottages and down Rectory Hill. The old embankment wall on the south side gives the road a combe-like atmosphere: the houses are set back behind solid sandstone walls, one being especially remarkable: Pillar House with a thatched portico on two cylindrical columns high above the road - a sort of Grand Thatched Cottage with gravitas. Rectory Hill ends at a junction facing Old Cleeve Farm. Turn right for Chapel Cleeve, Blue Anchor and the coast.

[91] *There is a beautiful way from Washford to Old Cleeve, best taken on foot, called 'The Monks' Path.' It follows the course monks from Cleeve Abbey walked to reach St. Andrew's church and then on to a chapel at Blue Anchor. The Path is still part-cobbled and tree-canopied, a home to an abundance of wild flowers. The summit is marked by the base of a wayside cross with views across the Bristol Channel to Steep Holm and Weston-super-Mare and a few other places...*

[92] *Owned by the Crown Estate, the orchard was threatened with development until the Prince of Wales intervened at the behest of Jeanne Webb in 1995. It is now maintained by the villagers for their use.*

There is a coastal footpath[93] from Watchet to Blue Anchor which begins at the holiday camp about 2 miles (3.2 km) up the hill out of the port. The path passes through several coastal woods and along field boundaries. You can also get down into Warren Bay. Due to erosion the cliff edge can be breathtakingly close to the path - so beware! Indeed the coastal border of one field has a semicircular area that has sagged 3 ft. (1 m) - likely to go any day! It's about here that Blue Anchor Bay emerges in the west and, with the mobile homes hidden, the hills above Dunster, in an Arcadian idyll of small woods and grassland, shelve gently to the sea.

On my 1809 map of the Somerset coast, the village of Blue Anchor[94] amounts to a cluster of dwellings at the eastward end of the bay, at the point where the Watchet road arrives at the beach. Although The Blue Anchor Inn still stands here, nowadays the village is found about a mile and a half along the coast, where the road turns inland for Carhampton. The arrival of the railway must have excited development here and the station dragged the name westward, along the shoreline. The railway station is a real period piece with a marvellous Great Western signal-box and a level-crossing with old style gates. If you're lucky, you may be soothingly delayed while a steam train pauses for passengers and then pulls away with a hoot and a shudder of steam.

The level crossing at Blue Anchor

[93]*According to Jeanne Webb, a little further inland from here, in Jenny Cridland's Copse, is the most westerly place in Great Britain where nightingales nest.*

[94]*The name seems to have arisen from boats mooring in the bay finding their anchors coated in blue clay. Robin Bush says that Blue Anchor Bay was once called Cleeve Bay although my 1809 map gives it no name at all - other than Blue Anchor village. According to Bush, the name was associated with an inn of that name, present as long ago as 1678. A Blue Anchor Inn was there when Charles Harper was writing in 1909. It still serves good ale.*

Gray Rock, Blue Anchor

Blue Anchor Bay makes a huge arc over 8 miles wide to Minehead, taking in Dunster Beach as it goes. Before the sea-wall was built, the low-lying central areas were marshy and vulnerable to flood. As you walk towards the eastern end of the bay, from the slipway that runs below the Blue Anchor Inn, the red cliffs change abruptly to the grey and greeny shales of the promontory Gray Rock.[95] This area is geologically famous for its exposure of Upper Triassic and Lower Jurassic rocks. When I was there (this place is changing all the time), fairly close to the promontory were great chunks of alabaster lying on the beach like lumps of discarded salmon-pink icing. Away from the cliffs, the tilted pavements were varicoloured with some of the stone filled with the fossils of small mussel-like shells.[96]

[95] *This is another fault-line where the younger shales have sunk to lie level with the older mudstones. The shales in the promontory are closely layered with crystalline inclusions. This is alabaster, a form of calcium sulphate or gypsum which, at Blue Anchor, can come in orange and vivid pinks. Or even white! It formed as successions of shallow, ancient seas dried up. It was once prized for ornamental work - Watchet alabaster has been used in some of the tomb carvings inside St. George's church, Dunster.*

[96] *Apparently, some of the beds here are fossil-rich with the remains of fish, bivalves and marine reptiles including the dolphin-like dinosaur; the Ichthyosaur (see Stogursey church example).*

The bay at Blue Anchor, late morning, low tide

The road separates Blue Anchor beach from fields set aside for caravans and camping and, in summer, this can be a busy place. At least the caravans come and go; whereas the mobile homes ("static caravans") just stay. The serried ranks of fierce white, rectilinear, shapes piled up on the hillside are so uncompromising and intrusive, and surely they don't need to be - the older style chalets in St. Audrie's and Dunster Beach are much gentler on the eye. How about some green camouflage!?

Looking north-west along the railway-line from the level-crossing gates, the pastoral mood returns with fields, the wooded hill of Conygar Tower, Dunster Castle and Minehead's North Hill. Away from the beach, Blue Anchor consists of 1920's houses set in generous gardens; sea-sidey and sedately suburban.

Up the gentle rise of Blue Anchor's Eastbury Hill (from which St. Andrew's Church at Old Cleeve is suddenly, vividly, visible), it's a short journey to Carhampton, painfully divided along the A39. St. John's Church is set back from the road amongst trees and one, a Japanese cherry close by the entrance porch, was in full, faded pink, bloom when I visited. Inside you are immediately struck by the beautiful carved screen painted in a tracery of blue, white and green, with detailing picked out in red.[97] The effect is delicate and luminous.

A short way along the road you come to The Junk Shop (subtitle: Chris's Crackers). This is an emporium that sells everything from abandoned fruit machines, neolithic (well all right; New Iron Age) farm implements, a frayed vaulting-horse or two, car jacks and flying ducks, as well as serious architectural salvage - and some less serious. It's the sort of place where you feel you are bound to find something you really need, or had forgotten you needed, or didn't know you had needed, but do now. Rosie and I came away with a 1920s London Underground poster and there can be no doubt that we needed it. Well, that's what Rosie said anyway.

[97]*Most church screens are dark and woody but this is a relatively recent innovation. I was told the repainting was carried out by daughters of the Luttrell family during the late 19th century. It is true to the medieval style.*

Gray Rock

Blue Anchor

10.20 am. Gray Rock with its alabaster cliffs then a sudden colour change to red. From the boat, Blue Anchor Bay swings away to Minehead's North Hill. Carhampton's red church tower visible above the rise of the beach. A train chuffs its way to Dunster Station leaving a trail of steam.

The West Somerset Railway

Start of the journey, Bishops Lydeard

In 1857, a group of West Somerset landowners got together to promote a new railway company. After its incorporation by Act of Parliament, the company announced that Isambard Kingdom Brunel had "consented to act as engineer." By September 1858 Brunel had mapped out the line and was ready to start but, through ill-health, probably played little part in the final design. Brunel's role was taken over by his principal assistant R.P. Brereton. Work began at Crowcombe in April 1859 and the whole line, from Taunton to Watchet, was completed in February 1862 - the first paying passengers enjoying the ride a few weeks later. The track was extended to Minehead in 1874.

At the start, the lines were Brunel's broad gauge track with management under the control of the Bristol and Exeter Railway - later absorbed by the Great Western Railway Company. Up until the Second World War the line made a reasonable profit but, in 1947, with nationalisation, British Railways took over and from then on services went into decline. The line just escaped Beeching's cuts in the 1960s but, by 1970, staff numbers had fallen to a sorry 11 and in January 1971 it closed. While all this was going on, a new West Somerset Railway Company (WSR) was riding to the rescue and in 1975, under the auspices of Somerset County Council, the company took over the line.

The new WSR runs from Bishops Lydeard, near Taunton, to Minehead and from the start has been hugely dependent on enthusiastic volunteers. The locomotives are both steam and diesel, nearly all in their original liveries (to the delight of 'traditionalists') and most of the passenger coaches date from the 1950s. Each of the stations along the 23 mile journey has its own charm and to travel the line is evocative and exciting.

From Bishops Lydeard the train climbs steadily, huffing and puffing along a valley that twists between the Brendon and Quantock Hills to reach the beautifully restored station at Crowcombe Heathfield. The line then slowly descends, to arrive at Stogumber where the station is perched on the hillside above the Railway Inn (now closed, but where I had a pork sandwich with my dad ages ago). The gentle descent continues to Williton and here the buildings and signal box are 'originals' dating from 1862. Then it's onto Watchet and the sea with the train skimming along the red cliffs of Doniford Bay. As the train enters Watchet you catch a glimpse of the harbour and the lighthouse. The station here is built at right angles to the track - a reminder that Watchet was the original terminus - the 'end of the line'. The train now begins its final climb, looping inland below St. Decuman's church (often lost in steam billowing from the paper mills) and bridging the defunct railtrack that once linked Watchet with iron ore mines in the Brendon Hills - 'The Mineral Line.'

At Washford station there's a small railway museum and the headquarters of the Somerset & Dorset Railway Trust - which once ran a branch line to Burnham-on-Sea. From here, a steep descent to the sea brings the train to Blue Anchor Bay where the line runs close to the beach. Blue Anchor station's 'down platform' waiting room is full of Great Western memories. The track from Blue Anchor to Minehead is almost level with prospects across the whole of Bridgwater Bay: north to the Welsh coast and over your shoulder to Brean Down and the Steep and Flat Holms.

The penultimate station is Dunster, a classy affair because the Luttrell family of Dunster Castle were involved in the line's extension to Minehead. Rail historian C. Van den Arend recounts that Mr. Luttrell had a Gold Pass which he kept on a chain. As he got onto the train he would exclaim;
"You have not asked to see my ticket!"
"We know you have a pass Sir." would come the reply.
"But I might have left it at home!" pressed Mr. Luttrell.
"We would still recognise you, Sir."

I wonder how often that jolly banter took place! There are no gold passes these days but the wonderful, real, 'Edmundson board' tickets, which are sold at all the station booking offices along the line, are printed at Dunster Station.

The journey ends, in little under 3 miles, at Minehead. The steam engine comes to halt close to the promenade with wooded North Hill and Higher Town before you in the north-west and the sea next door.

Chapter Thirteen

DUNSTER AND THE BEACH

Dunster Castle, from across the polo lawns

Dunster is beautiful. Almost too beautiful for its own good. The approach along the highway, crossing the pastures beyond Carhampton, is breathtaking. Dunster Castle and Conygar Tower stand on their separate wooded hills. Spread before them are the outstretched lawns of the estate and the backdrop of the silvan slopes of the Brendon Hills. It's a scene that demands the restful eye - difficult, as you are hurried along by the bustling A39.

And the small town maintains the delight. There is a discreet car-park close to the town entrance from which it's a few yards on foot into the main street. Rounding the corner, occupied by an age-old inn 'The Luttrell Arms', the village opens before you in a gentle swoop past the 16th century Yarn Market, chimneyed shops and houses, to the soft red sandstone of Dunster Castle on its wooded escarpment. Behind you, Conygar Tower,[98] from its leafy knoll, watches over the other end of the street. It's a scene of benign enclosure, almost domestic in its scale after the grand eastern approach across The Lawns.

The stables, Dunster Castle, winter sunlight

A castle has stood on Dunn's Tor[99] since 1086 at least, when William de Mohun moved in from Normandy. However, its present picture-book quality was the romantic creation of Anthony Salvin in 1872 for the Lord of the Manor: George Fownes Luttrell.[100] You enter the castle through its oldest part, a 13th century Gateway. Close by the entrance are some beautiful 17th century stables which double as a National Trust shop. Looking in from the doorway you will see the original stalls and boxes, their wonderfully turned stall-posts standing like a row of huge medieval skittles. North-facing windows allow an ethereal light to fall on the scene.

[98] Conygar Tower was built as a folly around 1760. It serves no function other than to be there and look amazing. It succeeds brilliantly. It's what declares Dunster to near and far.

[99] A tor is a rocky height. 'Dunn' may have been a Saxon noble.

[100] The castle was recast as a country house for a previous George Luttrell in about 1617. The architect was William Arnold who also designed Wadham College, Oxford and Montacute House, Somerset. The Luttrells had bought the De Mohun estate in 1375, although the De Mohun heirs later contested the transaction. The Luttrell family remained in possession until 1976 when Sir Walter Fownes Luttrell donated the castle to the National Trust.

Built around the old Gateway is a 15th century Gatehouse presenting a sombre
passageway into the castle grounds. This opens out into a splendid encircling terrace
which follows the southern aspect of the castle. Through the seasons different plants
are in flower - camellias, rambling roses, Angel's trumpets. I especially remember,
in late summer, a climbing shrub called Pileostegia (I asked a helpful gardener)
whose tiny white flowers scented the air by the steps to the South Terrace. An old
lemon tree still fruits in its personal glasshouse watched over by a wisteria below the
tower. The terrace then takes on a warm Mediterranean mood with an avenue of
Chusan palms defining its southern boundary. A flamingo fountain spills water into a
pool. Beyond the balcony wall the extraordinary vista extends, high above wide mown
lawns, to cloud shadows scurrying across the trees and hills opposite. Traffic threads
its way along the A39, while the eye moves on, following the curve of Blue Anchor Bay
to the blue-grey Severn Sea.

After all this light, entering the castle can seem claustral and dark, with drawn blinds and shading necessary to preserve furniture and fabrics. What you can see is a nice mixture of the baronial and the domestic. The lower floor consists of grand outer and inner halls, a dining room with a beautiful plaster ceiling. A great oak staircase rises from the inner hall to the upper floor where the rooms are much smaller in scale. Suddenly you move forward in time with what's alleged to be Somerset's first bathroom.[101] I wonder who had the second? And there's the surprise of an 'almost contemporary' 1930s bedroom belonging more in a London suburb. You don't expect that kind of thing in a castle.

The lemon tree

Also, it's the smaller details that are so appealing. Amongst the aristocratic knick-knacks I discovered, 'The Pollard Scentometer.' This consisted of a thermometer and a humidity gauge mounted with a circular slide rule. Apparently, this allowed you to calculate the probability of getting a scent for the hunt. Jolly good.

[101] *I like the story of the huge mahogany bath-cover. It was used to defend the decency of the bather in the event of a servant dropping by, etc. - it was moved by a pulley device. Well, the device failed and the cover dropped on Mrs Luttrell while she was in the bath - she escaped undamaged. I don't know about the bath-cover but it disappeared soon after, along with the defence of decency.*

Following the left turn, below the stables, takes you into West Street with more cobbled pavements, period houses and cottages. Mill Lane then continues on around the castle accompanied by the raised and channelled stream race that drives the two waterwheels of the Dunster Mill. Close by the River Avill flows. We have arrived in a beautifully designed setting of moving water and stone bridges that lead to wide open polo-lawns.[102] And a lot of Chinese rhubarb.

[102]*During the 1920s Dunster became the centre for polo in the West Country, entertaining fabulous Indian princes and players from America and Argentina. A pavilion was donated by the Maharajah of Jodhpur in 1925. It's still there.*

The monks' dovecote

Dunster's church of St. George began life as a priory church. The Benedictine priory vanished after the 1530s Dissolution but, amazingly, the monks' dovecote[103] and their tithe barn still stand. The 12th century dovecote is a lovely, simple, structure, a stone cylinder capped by a conical roof. The barn, with its imposing roofed entrance and ancient doors is close by. The barn provides one of the high walls that bound the Priory Gardens. Overlooked by the red sandstone Perpendicular tower of St. George, this wide grassy space and the smaller cloister garden are sanctuary from the tourist bustle.

The octagonal Yarn Market is testament to a time when Dunster's fortunes were dependent on a trade in wool and many of the local mills were involved in the finishing of woollen cloth.[104] The Luttrell Arms seems to have started life in the 15th century as a guest house for Cleeve Abbey, but by 1650 was an inn known as 'The Ship.' The main bar, with its huge fireplace, has a grand, rather churchy, window looking onto an internal courtyard. On cold days a scented log fire will be burning.

The courtyard, The Luttrell Arms

[103]*A machine for breeding pigeons, an important part of the Benedictine monks' diet. The Benedictines developed the cylindrical design with a cunning revolving ladder, borne by a central ash spindle (the 'potence' - French for 'gallows') which still, quietly and effortlessly, rotates on its old wrought-iron, 'pin and cone' bearings.*
Each breeding pair of pigeons would rear 2 young (squabs) every 3 weeks by which time, weighing 1 lb each, the squabs would be ready for the pie. This dovecote could produce 200 squabs a week! Lots for everyone.

[104]*A coarse woollen cloth was known as 'dunster.'*

'The Ship' is a clue to another of Dunster's important past histories. Early records reveal that it was a significant port or haven.[105] Indeed when King Stephen decided to bring William de Mohun, Lord of the Manor, to heel in 1139, he formed an army and marched on Dunster. When Stephen arrived, he disconsolately discovered a castle with "unconquerable fortifications... inaccessible on the one side because washed by the waves..." So he left a Henry de Tracy to sort William out.[106] Whether Dunster has ever been "washed by the waves" is doubtful, but during the 13th and 14th centuries Dunster Haven and Bridgwater were regarded as the two most important ports on the Somerset seaboard.

By the 17th century silt was causing severe problems for the port of Dunster and, despite its own silting difficulties, Minehead was beginning to filch all the trade. A hundred years later Dunster Haven had disappeared and all that was left was the River Avill forming a large loop (now called 'The Hawn') across the marshes, before it entered its tidal channel and the Severn Sea. It would be another century before Dunster Beach would be 'discovered.'

[105] According to marine historian John Gilman, the harbours or havens in this part
of the coast took the ancient form known as the 'weir harbour'.
These began as large ponds, often fed by a stream or spring,
that formed on the landward side of a shingle bank. The stream forced an exit through
the shingle which men then widened and made secure.
Such havens arose in Dunster, Carhampton, Watchet, Minehead and Porlock.
Often the haven decayed and disappeared, as in Dunster and Minehead.
Porlock remains a 'weir harbour' and is something of a rarity.

[106] During the Civil War, Robert Blake of Bridgwater and his Parliamentary army
also had problems dealing with Dunster Castle. Two years previously, in 1643,
it had been a parliamentary stronghold compelled to surrender to the Crown.
In June 1645 the future Charles II retreated to the castle for two weeks
and it wasn't until April 1646 that Blake's siege finally defeated the Royalists.
Cromwell later ordered the castle defences to be broken down.

Today, the expanded A39 junction separates the hamlet Marsh Street from the town. This part of Dunster feels quite different; it looks to the sea and the lowland slides gently to the coast. The exquisite Dunster Station, in its red brick livery and which once saw Mr. Luttrell and his Gold Pass, stands like a time capsule to an era long gone. When you arrive at the Beach the sensation of having slipped back to before the Second World War is even stronger. Rows of modest chalets[107] sit on a raised grass embankment above the high-water line. They are tidy, almost regimented, in the way they present themselves. Their small front windows look out to sea over tiny patios and verandas, where there's just enough room to put up a couple of deck-chairs. You can imagine the milk cart delivering milk by the measured Imperial pint into waiting jugs. The groceries at the Beach Shop. The butcher calling on Tuesdays and Fridays. The queues when the Fish and Chip van appeared twice a week. Water collected from standpipes along the beach. Primus stoves and paraffin lamps.

The Huts, Dunster Beach

[107]*At first the diminutive dwellings were called 'huts' and then, extraordinarily, for a while, 'bungalettes'!*
At times they have hurtfully been referred to as 'sheds.' 'Chalets' seems just about right. Though I still like 'huts.'

The first hut is supposed to have arrived in the early 1920s, having detached itself from Blue Anchor beach during a storm and embarked on a short voyage down the coast. The Luttrell estate then expanded the colony and by 1939 there were more than 160. The huts were built to a precise formula with dimensions 18 x 14 ft. Their original price was £65 and £75 for the veranda model, both in any colour provided it was green. They were positioned along the beach so as not to intrude on the sea-view from the castle.

During the Second World War the huts were requisitioned by the Army. With the break-up of the Luttrell estates in 1950, Dunster Beach acquired a new owner and became 'Hutlands'! A few years later the name moved upmarket as 'Beachlands.' In 1965 the Chalet Owners Association achieved a tenant buy-out so 'The Beach,' at last, belonged to the chalet owners themselves. These days the chalets are treasured family possessions and change hands for many thousands of pounds.

The Beach occupies the western end of Blue Anchor Bay and the pebble embankment soon gives way to fine shingle and sand. To the west, the sight line is limited by trees that proceed through the chalets to the shore forming a small wood that defends Dunster Beach from the Minehead Golf Course and Butlin's Holiday Camp.[108] To the east, the bay makes a majestic sweep to the Watchet bluff, then across Bridgwater Bay to the promontories of Brean Down and the built-up slopes of wooded Worlebury Hill. And behind all this, the Conygar Tower gazes benevolently down from a leafy fastness.

[108] There's a story that, in the early 1960s, Billy Butlin leant on the golf course fence and cast his eye over Dunster Beach as a possible site for his holiday camp. He considered it too constricted and so the camp sprang up west of the golf course. Phew...

Amongst the shingle and sand, plants abound. While we strolled through in late summer, Scentless mayweeds, with sunny-side up sort of flowers, were everywhere. Less brazen were the vigourous blue/pink spikes of Viper's-bugloss and the sunshine yellow of Evening primroses. On the higher pebbled ground and growing rather desperately was a lone tomato plant - a seed from somebody's sandwich? 'Gardener's Delight' perhaps, working hard to ripen five, small, green, fruit.

To the rear of the chalets is an area of cultivated water called 'The Hawn.' As mentioned earlier, this was the loop the River Avill once made before it entered the sea and may well be all that is left of the port of Dunster Haven. The Hawn now amounts to little more than an attractive backwater while a pipe diverts the Avill to the sea from the western end. The footbridge that spans The Hawn originally served as a flood-barrier; the arched housings for the floodgates are still there.[109] Storm and flood take their toll on the Beach. The high pebble embankment in front of the chalets is in a constant state of flux which has to be monitored and controlled. Gale-driven seas can remove huge quantities of sand and pebbles and the present timber groynes are an attempt to limit that. At the time of writing a system of sand capture and stabilisation with supported netting seems to be working. Hopefully all the defences will succeed so The Beach can survive as a paean to a way of holidaying that has almost disappeared.

[109] *The low land between Carhampton and Minehead has always been vulnerable to being "injured by the sea. In 1963 the Flood Relief Channel was cut from Loxhole Bridge near Dunster, diverting River Avill flood water to the eastern end of The Beach.*

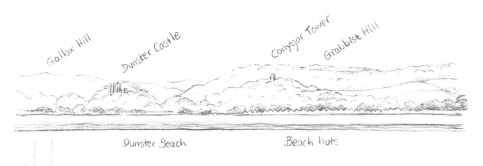

10.35 am. Moving speedily into Blue Anchor Bay. Red tower of Carhampton church. Patchwork of fields to Croydon Hill. Dunster Castle and Conygar Tower address the skyline with the Dunster Beach chalets scribbling along the shore.

Chapter Fourteen

MINEHEAD

The Sailor's Hobby-Horse, Wellington Square

It's May Day. As Rosie and I climb out of the car onto the Esplanade, we can hear the distant beating of a drum. The morning's sunny and dry and the Minehead Hobby-Horse will have been out and about, cavorting the streets and terrifying children, since 6 am. We follow the sound up The Avenue to the small square in front of the Wellington Hotel, where the Hobby-Horsemen are resting before the Horse's next gambol about the town. On one of the benches sits the melodeon player (a sort of accordion) showing a few rhythms and reels to a younger musician. The drummer, his big black drum (it may date from the 17th century) on the ground beside him, quietly sips a cola. The unoccupied Sailor's Horse waits patiently in the centre of the square.

To describe The Hobby-Horse is a little difficult, for it's like nothing else on earth. When occupied, it has the appearance of a clown sitting in a mobile bathtub filled to the brim with coloured rags and ribbons. The clown's head emerges from the ragbag with similar remnants masquerading as hair, a plume of jazzy ostrich feathers crowning the lot. A rim of white fur surrounds the white, tin face, scarlet nose and cheeks with spiky teeth. Below all this is a vast sacking skirt decorated with multicoloured bull's-eyes and a raggedy tail dangling from its rear end. The whole fantasy is supported on a willow withy frame.

To my astonishment, I'm invited to try the Horse for myself. On the inside, I discover the frame is carried by a shoulder harness, I push my head through that and then up into the mask. Inside, it smells a bit like a rugby changing room (I was warned) and my eyes don't quite line up with the eye-holes, increasing my sense of disorientation. Some of the frame's weight (one hundredweight or 51 kg) is carried by your arms; there are handholds so the whole animal grotesque can be lifted, tipped and swung from side to side. To animate the Hobby-Horse requires great skill and strength and it's extraordinary how its character can change; from being kindly and benign to a mood of high lunacy and threat.

We follow the Horse down the Avenue. The drummer beats a steady rhythmic march accompanied by the melodeon playing 'the hobby-horse tune' (otherwise known as 'Soldier's Joy'). The reception is wonderful. Huge grins and chortles when the Horse stoops and bows in thanks to a donation for charity. Children in pushchairs stare in apprehensive amazement, then smile with delight when reassured. People wave from doorways and hospital windows.

10.50 am. Bright white Butlin tents. Minehead moves up the wooded slopes of North Hill. Serrated hill-line of pines. From the sea, a crescent of open fields below Greenaleigh Farm. Heather blush on the hills.

The Original Sailor's Hobby-Horse

The origins of the Minehead Hobby-Horse are lost in antiquity, but there are tales
of it being used to frighten Vikings. There was a time, up to a hundred years ago,
hobby-horses featured in a number of May Day ceremonies throughout the British Isles.
Now only two have a true lineage; Minehead and Padstow, with Minehead folk
convinced the Cornish pinched the idea from them!

Years ago, the hobby-horse was more aggressive than it is now and was
equipped with wooden 'snappers,' covered with hare's skin.
With these, the Horse could snaffle passers-by and encourage a donation.
Recalcitrant donors could be held outstretched, face down, and whacked on their
behinds with a boot 10 times, each whack being accompanied with a bow from the horse.
This was called 'booting' and a version of it still occurs when the Horse visits Cher Steep,
on the outskirts of Minehead. The Hobby-Horse was also equipped with a real tail from
a genuine ex-cow and employed to thwack those reluctant to part with their money.
It must have become pretty disgusting as the days wore on.
Maybe it was disgusting to begin with.

The Sailor's Hobby-Horse emerges on the eve of May Day (April 30th)
at the pub 'The Old Ship Aground' on Minehead Quay. For the next three days the
Horse appears around Minehead and Dunster, raising money for local charities.
Traditionally, The Sailor's Horse has been based on The Quay.
Now and again a rival horse emerges and there are times when
May Day celebrations get a trifle heated.

The Higher Town, from the Promenade

When you come to Minehead by road or rail, the landscape is dominated by the high wooded hump of North Hill[110] standing guard over the north-west approaches to the harbour. On land and from the east, North Hill masquerades as a promontory, but from the sea the hill loses its definitive shape, merging with the high red sandstone cliffs of coastal Exmoor. These continue, so far as Somerset is concerned and excepting the 2 mile (3.2 km) interruption of Porlock Bay, to the Devon border and beyond. In old photographs of Minehead, North Hill is crosshatched with fields and hedgerows. Early in the 20th century, the fields were giving way to roads and villas - my old friend Charles Harper hated it and spent a lot of time grumbling about pickpockets. Fortunately the hotel and villa gardens have been enthusiastically planted with trees, so the hillside appears less developed than seemed inevitable a hundred years ago.

---

[110]*Like much of the hilly Exmoor coast, North Hill is made up from a Devonian rock called 'Hangman Sandstone,' predominantly red/purple/brown in colour but with some greys and greens. From North Hill to Glenthorne on the Somerset border, the Hangman Sandstone demonstrates fantastic faults and buckling caused by earth movements 300 million years ago. The Devonian Period spans from 405 - 355 million years ago.*

Traditionally 'old' Minehead is divided into three areas: Higher Town (or Church Town) clustered around St. Michael's Church up on the hill, Lower Town[111] at the bottom of the hill and Quay Town grouped about the harbour. The development of the resort has blurred things, but Higher Town and the Quay have retained some distinction. The name of the seafront variously called The Strand, Promenade etc., now seems settled to the older title of The Esplanade. In 1999 the Sea Defence Scheme was completed. This was made necessary by storms that had flooded parts of the town earlier in the decade.[112] Storms have blighted the Minehead seaboard with painful regularity over the centuries and the 1999 defences are the first substantial attempt to stabilise this part of the coastline.

The 1999 sea-wall is a truly impressive construction of precast concrete. The massive cappings are concaved seaward to reflect the incoming waves (as in Burnham-on-Sea) and faced on the landward side with Old Red sandstone. Large boulders of Mendip Carboniferous limestone protect the wall's footings.[113] The entire structure gives the impression of being 'over-engineered' - in the best Victorian sense. At the same time, the wall is really comfortable to lean against, arms stretched out over the domed top, warmed in the sun, gazing out to sea.

[111]*In 1791 a fire that started with a burning barrel of pitch in Bampton Street ended up destroying much of the prosperous Lower Town. The Mr. Luttrell of the time failed to rebuild and even 5 years later Minehead presented "a vast number of houses in a state of blackened ruin and dilapidation". It would be 30 years before the town recovered.*

[112]*The original sea-wall had been built in 1901 and before that the seafront had consisted of a shingle ridge defended by wooden piles, a footpath skirting the top. In 1910 a Great Storm destroyed much of the Victorian sea defences and badly damaged cottages in Quay Town.*

[113]*Are the Mendips moving to the West Somerset coast?*

The wall has imposed a satisfying unity on the seafront. Butlin's donated part of the promenade it owned, allowing the scheme to take in the entire sweep of the bay, from the golf course in the east, to the harbour in the west. David Brown's Sundial[114] is an intriguing diversion as you stroll the promenade near The Avenue junction. Close by, on the other side of the road, West Somerset Railway steam trains pull up at the long platform of Minehead Station - the end of the line, all the way from Bishops Lydeard.

A shelter of ladies

The Avenue, which has managed to hold on to its precious Lime trees, runs straight into the centre of the town. It's mostly a late 19th century development linked to the arrival of the railway. The houses, built of red sandstone, began life as guest-houses and small hotels. Today, most of the front gardens and ground floors are given over to shops and cafes. There's a strong whiff of chips upon the air. Running off The Avenue are attractive roads of small terraced Victorian houses. They too are constructed from local stone which harmonises with the grander buildings of the Avenue and the Parade.

[114]*Commissioned in 2002 to celebrate Queen Elizabeth II's Golden Jubilee. The sundial is built into the promenade pavement, with York stone and brick paviers marking out the compass points, the hours and a central date scale. This is an analemmatic (?) sundial, where you, standing as the central marker, have to move along the centre line each month through the year. Your shadow tells the time of day on the ground before you. Brilliant.*

Wellington Square occupies the heart of the old Lower Town and was the place where the stagecoaches, from Taunton, Bridgwater and Lynmouth, would arrive and depart. Two inns were in fierce competition here during the early 19th century - the upstart 'Wellington Hotel' and the older 'Plume of Feathers.' The upstart still stands but the handsome Plume of Feathers, which once filled the western side of the square, was inexplicably demolished in 1966, to be replaced by a block of staggering awfulness. The day is saved in Park Street (which runs off the square) where butchers Gerald David & Sons' have a breathtaking display of Exmoor meat filling their shop window. Round the corner, in Parks Lane are some fine Georgian and Victorian terraces. On one corner is a magnificent Victorian Gothic house, in beautiful sandstone, called Mentone Villa. I could live there.

Back towards the seafront and west of the Avenue is Blenheim Gardens, a reassuringly typical municipal park of lawns and blazing flower beds. It has a fine collection of broadleaf trees. West Somerset Council has done well for itself by occupying the terrace in Blenheim Road overlooking the Gardens. A most salubrious location.

Leaving the park, it's a few steps back onto the promenade where, from this end of the bay, the dazzling white tents of the Butlin pavilions fills the eastern landscape. Billy Butlin arrived in May 1962, setting up camp on the marshy ground next to Warren Point and Madbrain Sands. Families stayed in chalets and ate in a huge communal hall.[115] In the 1980s the Rank Organisation took over and updated the whole concept and it became 'Somerwest World.' It has to be said, with the arrival of Butlin's Minehead lost its innocence and aspirations of gentility. It has stretched the social resources of the town in many ways, something the high-rise developments along the Warren Road seafront are likely to compound.

[115]*I have to admit to an interest here. In 1968 I worked for a month as a locum doctor at the camp. Just as I arrived, the place hit the national headlines with a rampant tyre slasher in the camp car-park. I was kept busy by campers seeking a second opinion to their own GP about their various disorders. It seemed expected as part of what Butlin's had to offer! But what really impressed me was the Tropical Typhoon Jungle Bar, where a storm, complete with thunder, lightning and torrential rain, was turned on every half hour.*

Turning to the west, the Esplanade now becomes Quay Street leading to the harbour. Close to the junction with Blenheim Road is a row of red sandstone Coastguard cottages set back in deep front gardens. Cordyline palms impart a Mediterranean air. Behind rise the bosky slopes of North Hill, well tenanted with houses and hotels hiding amongst the trees. The wider part of Quay Street was once filled with cottages, their backyards to the sea.[116] In some parts, extension of the promenade has raised the road above the entrances to the surviving cottages. Facing the harbour, doorways need the protection of slotted boards should the tide decide to call. This is a wonderful part of the town where the cots press tight around the base of the hill and look out over the harbour to the protective arm of the north pier.

[116]*The story is that they were badly damaged in a 1910 storm, although it wasn't until the early 1920s they were demolished to make way for a wider promenade.*

The Harbour at Minehead

Minehead's harbour (a 'weir harbour') began with a small creek at the mouth of the Bratton Stream which once flowed in the direction of the Parade (then called Puddle Street). A port was first mentioned in 1380. By the mid-16th century it was protected by a small jetty at the north-east point of the hill. Even then the weir harbour managed to shelter ships of over 70 tons and Minehead had become an important port. Merchants based in the town traded as far as the Continent and West Indies and built their homes and warehouses in the Lower Town. In 1616 George Luttrell constructed a new harbour pier which brought added prosperity but over the next hundred years the port battled with the build up of pebbles and silt. By 1716 a further 100 ft. (30.4 m) of stone pier had been added by Dorothy Luttrell - achieved despite a crooked contractor and a storm that smashed much of the new work as well as houses in Quay Street.

The town continued to prosper for most of the 18th century with trade in wool, linen, oak-bark, hides, herrings, and culm coal for lime burning, to mention a few. Throughout this time the fight to keep the harbour clear of stones was gradually being lost. The shallow depth of water meant that large ships could no longer use the port and high charges also drove trade away.

By 1792 Ilfracombe was moving into ascendancy. At the start of the 1700s, forty ships were trading between Ireland and Minehead. At the century's end it was down to five or six. But all was not lost, the town had been noticed and "Persons of fashion have been to visit it as a bathing place in the summer season." Minehead's tide was turning in a different sort of way.

Viewed from within the harbour, much of the stone north pier is as the Luttrells left it. When 'The Pier Hotel' (later to become 'The Old Ship Aground') was built at the turn of 1900, many of the old storehouses, shipbuilding yards and dwellings were demolished. All except the small chapel of St. Peter on the Quay[117] which still stands next to the hotel.

Minehead harbour

Some of the harbour wall was rebuilt at the same time as the construction of The Pier Hotel - the curve of neat masonry above the slipway betrays it. Further along, there are massive stones belonging to the original pier and its 1716 extension. Old boulders are evident in the first part of the wall on the seaward side as well. The steep steps into the harbour seem truly ancient and straight out of Treasure Island, while the pierhead and the concrete facings on the seaward side of the harbour wall belong to the late 20th century; efficient, but no romance.

[117]*Previously the 'Inner Sellers' (store cellars) left to the town in 1630 by Robert Quirke, in gratitude for surviving a storm at sea. It provided funds for the almshouses he built in the town, which survive close to the Parade - "...and curssed be that man that shall convert it to any other use than for the use of the Poore 1630." Hopefully, the conversion to a chapel has side-stepped the malediction!*

Other than boat-hire for line fishing, there is little professional fishing from the harbour. Craft like the 'Defiant,' 'Ark Supreme' and 'Shalimar' are kept busy at weekends and during the holiday season. There is still one registered fishing boat: the small green hulled 'Ortac - BD·99.' But she does little of the real stuff these days, I was told.

The Old Ship Aground is a becoming, slate roofed, Victorian hotel and pub. Its bay windows look across the harbour and along Quay Street and its original name was linked to the

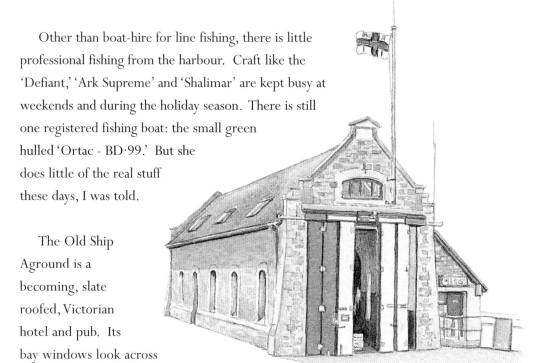

The Lifeboat House

construction of an iron pier (1901)[118] - which reached out 250 yards (229 m) into the sea from close to where the Lifeboat House now stands. The concrete supports and twisted ironwork can still be seen at low tide. Minehead's lifeboat[119] and its station house also arrived in 1901. The beautifully maintained station is built of red sandstone with high red doors and an Atlantic 21 lifeboat on show. Only a few weeks before Rosie and I were there, a fishing boat with 3 crew (and 1 dog) had been rescued in rough seas.

[118]*By 1901 this area of the harbour had lost most of its very old buildings including an ancient hostelry 'The New Inn' which stood opposite the 'Pier Hotel.' Even before the new iron pier, steamers were unloading 1,500 trippers a day. During the Second World War, the pier was dismantled because it supposedly obstructed a harbour gun-emplacement. Not long after the pier disappeared, the gun did too!*

[119]*In 1901 a 35' Liverpool class lifeboat, the 'George Leicester' was installed. Today, five lifeboats later, the station has a 24' Atlantic 21 rigid inflatable craft with a back-up D-class inflatable.*

Immediately behind the Lifeboat House, a tarmac path continues under the brow of the hill beside a mown meadow of 'made ground' and a bank high with Alexanders and Green alkanet. The trees of North Hill cascade to the shoreline above the pebbled ridge and almost immediately, the track (George Luttrell's Marine Walk) dives under them, coursing its way to Greenaleigh Sand. Going that way takes you to the base of Culver Cliffs, rising from the shore some 90 ft (27 m). This is the Hangman Sandstone which underlies much of Exmoor (see footnote earlier in this chapter); the red rock, folded by almost 90°, seems impossibly contorted - this folding becomes even more dramatic further down the coast.

The start of the South West Coast Path

'Jack Hammer,' St. Michael's Church

Back at Quay Street, on its seaward side, the South West Coast Path[120] both begins and ends. The terminus is marked by a great pair of galvanised steel hands holding a map, while across the street, the path zigzags uphill through the trees and houses.

The Coastal Path soon cuts westwards through the trees, but following Church Path takes you past the wonderfully sited War Memorial and views beyond Dunster and the Brendon Hills, a place to sit and remember. St. Michael's Road leads through an area called The Cross (the crossing of roads from the harbour and the town) with terraced cottages, some of which started life as small barns. This was the poorer area of the town.[121]

The church, with its lychgate standing above the road on a raised pavement, is little changed over hundreds of years. St. Michael's tower is constructed of Blue Lias limestone with buttresses of red sandstone - elements in the geology over which it presides. Inside, peering down from the great rood screen, is the slightly sinister figure of a boy in a green tunic and a red cap. He's 'Jack Hammer,' part of the original striking mechanism, and all that remains, of a 17th century church wall clock.[122]

[120]The Coast Path runs from Minehead to Lands End and then on to Poole Harbour in Dorset, a distance of 615 miles (992 km). The steel hands were designed by a local 'A' level student Sarah Ward and fashioned by sculptor Owen Cunningham.

[121]In 1800 the Revd. Richard Warner said the Higher Town "had nothing to recommend its shabby, irregular lanes..." but he did like the views.

[122]The church is also famed for a beautiful 15th century illuminated prayer book, 'The Missal of Richard Fitzjames.' He was vicar of St. Michael's from 1485 - 1497.

Eastward from below North Hill

Below St. Michael's, the Church Steps fold their way between whitewashed, thatched cottages. The steps end at a red sandstone building once known as 'Punter's Tenement' which was Minehead's Poorhouse back in 1731. A short way south, along Vicarage Road, a stream suddenly bubbles from the side of 'Riverside Cottage,' only to immediately disappear. It re-emerges further down the hill in Middle Street, flowing along a ferny open channel towards St. Michael's School. It then goes missing again, making a final appearance (so far as I know) off Holloway Street, gurgling beside a footpath to Hayman Road.[123]

[123]*This unnamed brook arises on the North Hill and first presents itself above Moor Road in the combe below Moor Wood. It then flows through private land, making a public appearance, complete with stepping stones, in Pemswell Lane before its arrival at Riverside Cottage. After Holloway Street, it joins the Bratton Water in its culvert beneath Blenheim Gardens. In 1890 the Bratton Water was still flowing through the town and flooding from time to time.*

Chapter Fifteen

NORTH HILL TO HURLSTONE POINT

Greenaleigh Farm

Directly opposite the Galvanised Hands on Minehead's Quay Street, the South West
Coast Path dives between the hill-hugging cottages to a path that zigzags up through
the trees. In the late 19th century George Luttrell laid out many scenic excursions
over North Hill with routes heading off in various directions. One favoured destination
was Greenaleigh Farm, about 1.5 miles (2.4 km) north-west from Minehead Harbour.
The previously described Marine Walk skirts the shoreline to Greenaleigh, but the

Coast Path takes on a gentle acclivity amongst the trees with "charming prospects" of the harbour below. The track here is quite wide and originally designed to accommodate a small horse and cart[124] taking visitors for tea at Greenaleigh Farm. The Coast Path soon dips to join the shoreline route above the farm's pastureland. This whole area, called Greenaleigh Point and now owned by The National Trust, is the only coast-level meadowland between Minehead and Porlock Bay.

From the sea, the pasture presents as a large, gently sloping, grassy semicircle below the treeline, reaching to the protective shingle ridge of the shore with the farm buildings set back against the trees. As with all National Trust property the farm looks well cared for although, even in the 19th and early 20th centuries, it was a successful Cream Tea enterprise and, between the wars, was famed for its own ice-cream.[125] In the fields below the farmhouse, which when we arrived on the Coast Path we found fell away quite steeply to the shore - the appearance from the sea is an illusion - dark cattle grazed. The pathway passes between the farm buildings and narrows to a simple track which soon divides; the Coast Path moves along uphill, but the lower route traces its way to the ruined and secretive 'Burgundy Chapel,'[126] tucked away at the bottom of its own combe.

[124]Even so it wasn't without hazard; the drop over Culver Cliffs was only protected by a rickety wooden fence with no defending trees on the slopes. It must have been the 'Terror Ride' of its day and genuinely dangerous.

[125]According to writer Brian Pearce, ice had to be transported from Dunster for the ice-cream making. And a certain John Page described Greenaleigh Farm as being "devoted in summertime to the high revel of junketing parties...."

[126]The remains of a medieval chapel attached to an earlier domestic building - possibly a hermitage. They are built from local red sandstone and there's some evidence of terraces, above the cliffs, for growing crops. Conceivably it was erected by a member of the Luttrell family upon his safe return from the Burgundian Wars in the 14th century. Peter Hesp speculates that it became a depository for Minehead longshoremen's contraband wine and was named after a boat, on passage from Burgundy, wrecked on rocks 2 miles from home. Another explanation holds it was a 'chapel-of-ease' serving the lonely hill farms, its name being a corruption of Byrcombe. I'll go for the second story!

The coastal track stops here. To regain the South West Path you have a simple choice; you can either backtrack and follow the upper route, or take a deep breath and ascend the steep Burgundy Chapel Combe. It is very steep. And a bit crumbly at the beginning. About half way up my legs went wobbly and insisted I lie back on the grassy slope for 10 minutes or so. But believe me it's well worth it... if you can still breath that is.

Burgundy Chapel Combe and the wobbly legs

At the top of the combe, you are well clear of the treeline with the blue-grey expanse of the Severn Sea below. Joining the main track for just under a mile, the National Trust then offers a choice of route: 'The Rugged Coastal Path' - through a gate and down into Grexy Combe or 'The Official South West Coast Path' - which moves gently westward. If you've just come up Burgundy Chapel Combe think twice about The Rugged Path (which sounds evangelical); it's likely to finish you off for the day. But it is very beautiful... and rugged.

The rugged route immediately plunges down a broken track into the eastern head of Grexy Combe. As you descend you become aware there are also southern and western heads and at the combe floor, a small confluence of their three streams. Crossing the streams, the path immediately rises along the west side of the combe with the Iron Age enclosure, Furzebury Brake, above you at the top of the climb. It's well named because you can't see anything for the furze. As you round the Brake, the coastline opens out, headlands curving steeply 720 ft (220m), down to the pebbly shore. We could hear the whoosh of the breaking waves. To the west you can see the shingle ridge of Greenaleigh Point with its small landward lagoon and just an edge of pastureland. The way is easier now, meandering alongside a turfy dry-stone wall that snakes away along the contours of the headlands like Hadrian's Wall.

In warm late May there was a fever of vegetative activity: bracken fronds were unfurling, coiled like tensioned springs, small intense bluebells, the white flowering of elder and mountain ash; red-purple foxgloves in vertical groups along the path or against the stone wall. Whortleberry, making fresh pink-green growth, covered the upper slopes. In places the cliffs had fractured and slipped, forming less vertiginous areas of lumpy ground[127] where ash and mountain-ash have managed to take hold. After this easy bit, the path descends once more, this time fringing the pasture of West Myne, down into Henners Combe where another stream courses its way to the sea. It's then a steady climb to the head of East Combe and on upwards to rejoin the official path, or westwards to Hurlstone Point.

The rugged path

[127] *These are called the Eastern and Western Brockholes. What's a brockhole? 'Brocc' is Old English for badger so perhaps there were setts here - although badgers usually favour woodland. According to the OED, 'brockle' is broken pieces, fragments, rubbish - which describes the terrain perfectly. So maybe it's the Somerset dialect again.*

From Burgundy Chapel Combe, the Official Coast Path continues along a relaxed route, bordering the grazing land of East and West Myne.[128] It is gentle now, following the easy undulation of the moor with tracks disappearing into the tall gorse from time to time. The high pasture extends up to the coastal bluffs - when we passed; manicured and mown with the precision of Lord's Cricket Ground. Patches of gorse illuminate the soft curves of the fields, with clusters of trees in sheltered gulleys where small streams run. Although it was dry when Rosie and I walked this way in early Spring (midway during a seven week spell of sunny weather), there were places where channels had been cut through the banks along the rough roadway so storm-water could run off the track into neighbouring fields. Some of these were damp, fed by tiny rivulets, despite the drought. Along the way were several wide areas where gorse fires[129] had taken hold, as though the blaze of colour had provoked its own combustion. From a distance they appeared scorched and dead but close to, bright green life was emerging.

The elevated path ends just below Selworthy Beacon, where the track falls away through the furze to Hurlstone Point. Before us lay Porlock Bay, curving against a glittering green-blue sea to the recurring headlands of Gore and Glenthorne and on, beyond the Somerset border, to Desolation and Foreland Point.[130] Inland, the prospect was equally heart stopping; the lush Vale of Porlock stepping back from low coastal meadows. Part obscured by Bossington Hill, we could see a coverlet of fields moving southwards along the broad valley and the rise of Exmoor above Horner Wood. We sat here for a while, avoiding a cool northerly wind by ducking below the gorse and getting round Thermos coffee, cheese and Marmite sandwiches rounded off with some chewy Tunnock's Caramel Wafer Biscuits.[131]

[128] These were once separate farms but they were abandoned during the Second World War. The land is now owned and managed by the National Trust.

[129] Many are controlled burns to sustain the variety of the Maritime Heath. The Heath consists of - Western gorse; Ulex galii (which flowers in late summer), Gorse; Ulex europaeus (which flowers at any old time - see Steart chapter), Bell heather, whortleberry, Bristle bent grass....it's a unique flora.

[130] These are all 'hog's-back' cliffs, characterised by a long slope towards the sea ending in a relatively small cliff above the shore.

[131] The wrapper says: "4,000,000 made and sold every week." 4 million!?!

From the top of Hurlstone Point there are two tracks running east and west of the promontory. The easterly route takes you down a steep scree slope to meet a land-slipped path running from the ruined Coast Guard lookout on the Point. The west track descends treeless Hurlstone Combe with Bossington Beach far below. This is the route of the South West Coast Path which then follows the lower contours of Bossington Hill into Bossington itself.

Hurlstone Point

Foreland Point

Approaching Hurlstone Point

11.30 am. The wind has dropped, engine on. We sail past the combes on
'the rugged path,' the collapsed ground of the Eastern and Western Brockholes appears crumpled from the sea.
Foreland Point emerges beyond Hurlstone, damson blue

Chapter Sixteen

SELWORTHY, ALLERFORD AND BOSSINGTON

Selworthy Green, looking to Dunkery Hill

The A39 runs through Minehead away from the coast, swerving past the villages
of Woodcombe and Bratton which now occupy the western outskirts of the town.
The road then passes along a beautiful high valley between North Hill and Periton Hill,
to descend slowly along the side of the Porlock Vale below Bossington Hill where,
after a few miles, you take the right hand turn for Selworthy.

The road climbs a fairly steep 1:4 hill with the village well hidden behind the tunnel
of trees. Eventually, the road surfaces at Selworthy's whitewashed Church of All Saints.
It occupies a heavenly spot. Lifted above the road on a small escarpment, All Saints looks

out over the entrancing sweep of the Vale of Porlock.[132] What you see is much of the Holnicote Estate (12,500 acres, given to the National Trust by Sir Richard Acland in 1944), an 11th century manor with small beautiful villages, farmland and ancient woodland, from the sandstone coastline between Minehead's North Hill and Bossington Beach to the high moorland of Dunkery Hill. This is a rare landscape because the Trust has sustained its context and the precious relationship of the people who live and work on the land. It's somehow confirming. It's how you want England to be... everywhere.

Down in the valley below Selworthy church, looking out over the tree canopy, the wide fields fold and overlap, their margins stalked by lone, magisterial oaks and clumps of gathering woodland. The scene has a viridian intensity eased by the passing drift of cloud shadows. For a moment a copse or church tower will assume centre stage, picked out in sunlight then, within an instant, it slips back into anonymity. The broad bands of pasture occupy most of the valley floor, rolling east and west. Almost due south, across the valley, the village of Luccombe sits amongst its Copper beeches as the land lifts again. Behind, two small combes move up through the woods of the Luccombe Plantation to where the trees give way to moorland. There, the muffled purple-brown moors scale the slopes of Dunkery Hill to Dunkery Beacon.[133]

Along with the view from its porch, All Saints is famed for its south aisle, a sort of 16th century ecclesiastic extension. It has a high wagon roof, two south and one east-facing windows; with their generous size and elegant stone tracery, they flood the interior with light. Inside the small tower is a 400 year old clock which instructs the village of the hour by striking the tenor bell - there is no clock face. Just as old is a crumbling parish chest, its wood is slowly disappearing, leaving its ironwork with nothing to defend

[132]*Curiously, we are back with the Blue Lias. The Selworthy side of the Vale of Porlock is the only place on Exmoor where it is found. Below All Saints' Church, at Buddle Hill, the limestone was once quarried from pits.*

[133]*At 1,703 ft (519 m) Dunkery Beacon is (excluding man-made extensions) Somerset and Exmoor's highest point. It was gifted to the National Trust in 1932 by Lt-Colonel Walter Wiggin. As its name describes, it was the site of beacon-fires lit "to alarm the country in times of civil discord or foreign invasion." In Luccombe, it was the custom to climb the Beacon on Easter Sunday to watch the sun rise, thus assuring good fortune for the coming year.*

*Limewashing
at Allerford*

Yellow ochre limewash

Tearing ourselves away from the vista and past the Preaching Cross, a small gate allows access into Selworthy.[134] as though we were slipping into someone's back garden. The small, thatched, Postman's Cottage exhales a soft smell of wood-smoke. A stream runs by. The Green with its setting of pale, yellow-ochre, limewashed cottages is a scene of inescapable charm.[135]

Although it is enclosed by high woods, the way the land falls gives sight lines to Dunkery Hill, while in the near ground there is a cadence of thatched roofs and chimneys. You sit there and think; "This cannot possibly be true…"

[134]In 1828 Sir Thomas Dyke Acland adapted the village's medieval farmhouses and buildings to a fashionable, rusticated, style; complete with outside loos. By removing stables, paddocks and yards he formed the Green. The cottages were then let to farm workers and retired servants of the estate.

[135]The yellow ochre limewash is the Holnicote Estate signature for its older buildings. The church is different it is coated with a weather protective mixture of white lime and tallow. At one time most of the churches in West Somerset would have looked the same.

Selworthy lies under the lee of Bossington Hill, below Selworthy Beacon. Rosie and I crossed the stream and climbed up through the woods (planted by Thomas Acland to welcome the birth of each of his children) to the Iron Age camp of Bury Castle. This is a pleasant place of hummocks and grassy mounds. Just beyond, in a grove of Scot's pine, stands the sandstone Wind and Weather Hut. The Acland family had romance coursing their veins. Thomas died in 1871, but his son John chose the spot where the hut would stand, 'In Remembrance' of his father. Some of the walls are inscribed with verse by John Keble[136] and Reginald Heber which, for me, hasn't worn so well as the hut.

From the poems, it's a short walk to the Selworthy Beacon (marked by a disappointing pile of stones) where fires were lit to warn the district of the advancing Spanish Armada. These days, ignition takes place at times of celebration like the 50th anniversary of the close of the Second World War, royal jubilees and weddings. Close by, runs the South West Coast Path (and the steep trip down Hurlstone Combe) with fantastic vistas across Porlock Bay to Glenthorne and Foreland Point.

Back on the A39, and a little further north-west, are the hamlets of Allerford and Bossington. Like Selworthy, they lie under the protection of woody Bossington Hill. The diminutive River Aller rises in the hills and combes around Wootton Courtenay, to flow across the Vale of Porlock. Coursing through Allerford, it is crossed, close to the ford, by a beautiful, narrow, low-arched, packhorse bridge guarded by the red sandstone Bridge Cottage, with its porch on stilts. For a while the road accompanies the river through the village, past soft, yellow, Holnicote cottages (terracotta roof tiles here) overlooked by the woods of Allerford Combe. Tucked away in the old village school is the delightful Rural Life Museum which comes with all the intriguing clutter of a vanished way of life. The Victorian schoolroom is there; ranks of ingrained desks, inkwells and benches. Not so Victorian either - it's redolent of the church school I went to in the early 1950s.

---

[136]*John Keble (1792-1866) was Professor of Poetry at Oxford. Oxford University's Keble College was established 3 years after his death. Reginald Heber (1783-1826) became Bishop of Calcutta in 1823.*

The road moves on towards the coast, passing by the small settlements of Lynch and West Lynch. Just west of here, the Aller joins the stream called Horner Water (which springs up around Dunkery Hill) to run on through Bossington and the short mile to the sea. In spring and summer all these villages are a riot of roses, woodbine, red valerian, blue garden geraniums, fig trees with their figs... Bossington was once known for its walnut trees (Harper described one as having a trunk circumference of 16 ft/4.9 m). There are still several elderly specimens on Bossington Green, close to the entrance to the village. They're now accompanied by a few youngsters replacing lost trees -

Bossington

one I thought to be a Black walnut; a North American for heaven's sake! Along the footpath in the fields above Bossington there are several great walnut trees of some seniority. When we were there in early June the baby nuts were coming up ready for pickling.[137]

Bossington is the archetypical West Somerset village, blessed in having been isolated by especially narrow country roads. The main street has a satisfying twist to it with a congenial mix of tiled and thatched houses and cottages. Most have the characteristic high pillar chimneys which front the building onto the street, with their base incorporating a bread oven. The height of the chimneys improved the up-draught to the fire, reducing the likelihood of smoke blow-back. It must also have minimised the risk of sparks setting fire to the thatch.

[137] *My grandmother pickled walnuts. You have to get them before the nutshell forms.*
The baby walnuts are pricked all over but beware; the black stain is impossible to get rid of and it has to wear off.
Even worse than whortleberries! They're soaked in brine (twice), dried and then bottled with spiced malt vinegar.
They're coal black, look deadly and they're delicious.

Lime-kilns and Lime

Lime kilns on Bossington Beach

All along the West Somerset coastline we came upon lime-kiln ruins; bulbous, stone, chambers with chimneys, used for the production of quicklime by burning limestone with coal. Often they were built into a bank or a cliff-face and had become stranded by tidal erosion; others were free-standing blockhouses, cavernous and dank, sprouting ferns.

In West Somerset, limestone was not so freely available as in other regions of the county. Here, much of the special stone, from Lilstock to Watchet, was gathered on beaches where various limestone strata were exposed (they still are). West of Watchet, beach limestone was even more difficult to obtain, and so was imported from Aberthaw on the Welsh south coast. The other vital ingredient was Welsh culm, a cheap, impure, coal-dust left over from mining coal.

Building the kiln into a cliff face simplified its construction. As well as supporting and insulating the structure, it was fairly straightforward to construct a ramp in order to fill it. The kiln was loaded via the chimney with alternating layers of limestone and culm. At the base of the kiln was a 'draw-hole' which allowed air into the firing chamber and the extraction of the quicklime when the 'burning' was complete. Although they varied in design, this was the basic system of the so-called 'draw kiln.' Draw kilns could be kept continuously fired by adding more fuel and limestone through the chimney. Earlier kilns ('flare kilns') did a single burn and had to be reloaded.

Continued

Continued from over

Landing and unloading the heavy materials was a dangerous business for the sailors
who ran their smacks and ketches, back and forth, across the Severn Sea.
A change in the wind could leave boats stranded, to break their backs on the open beaches.
A strong onshore wind could make it impossible to beat off the beach with craft
driven onto the rocks and wrecked. Men lost their lives.

The heat from the burning culm made the limestone (a form of calcium carbonate)
break down into calcium oxide (quicklime) and carbon dioxide (which went up the chimney to
contribute to greenhouse gases). Quicklime reacted with water to form slaked-lime
(calcium hydroxide). The various forms of 'lime' have different uses.
Limestone (unburned!) was a fine building material and slaked-lime used to make mortar.
Limestone, from the Lias stratas east of Watchet, contained added silica and
alumina in the shales. With burning, it formed 'hydraulic' lime, capable of making
a mortar that hardened under water. Lime from Watchet was used to build the
Eddystone Lighthouse in 1759. On the acidic soils of Quantock and Exmoor, lime's alkaline
properties were used to improve fertility. Slaked lime and water made limewash for painting
walls. When quicklime reacted with water, it generated enormous heat and was thrown onto
corpses in times of 'plague and pestilence' in an attempt at disinfection.

There's a small car-park at the seaward end of the village where Horner Water,
momentarily, breaks cover from the woods below Bossington Hill. We crossed the
stream by the wooden bridge and followed the track, through the sycamore woods,
along its east bank, before ascending the gentle contour of the hill away from the
pastures of the plain. Meanwhile, Horner Water continued to the sea. Sheep grazed
the wide, green, fields below us and our easy climb continued across the foot of
Hurlstone Combe to the headland of Hurlstone Point. The slopes here were covered
with the same maritime heath we had encountered on North Hill and around the
Selworthy and Bossington Beacons - all now 300 ft (91 m) above us. In areas where
grasses prevailed, clusters of pink thrift toughed it out. At our feet grew mounds of
raggedy, white-petalled sea campions, with their peculiar, veined, bladders puffed up
behind their flowers; all nodding, head-heavy, in the wind. In mid-June, the path was
perfumed with calmative honeysuckle and dog rose.

As we climbed, the dusky stone former Coastguard Station[138] peered down over the edge of the headland. Though roofless and abandoned, it retains the strength of its fine masonry, which the Victorians had brought to even this lonely spot. From its high windows, it still commands the same imperious view across a greeny Severn Sea (Rosie says that it's cobalt green - with touches of pale viridian!). From the lookout, we could see straight down the great, grey, arc of Porlock Bay's shingle ridge and the colour change of the salt-stained pasture where the sea had broken through (see Special Page: 'Porlock Bay and the Shingle Ridge'). Above Porlock, the wooded slopes give way to high pasture, while the woods themselves continue as a dark green band to the coast. Indentations in the canopy betray the presence of small combes as the trees encircle the pocket-sized harbour of Porlock Weir.

[138] *The 1902 Coastguard Station was still manned during the Second World War. At that time, its roof had to be reinforced to protect it from the heavy military ordnance being used on the slopes above. The building looks fairly intact - it doesn't appear that the roof was blown away by 'friendly fire.'*

Chapter Seventeen

PORLOCK BAY

Bossington Beach

Below Hurlstone Point, at the elbow of the promontory, a narrow and steep path takes you down through the bracken into Porlock Bay. You land at an area known as Bossington Beach, made extraordinary by the famous 'Shingle Ridge.' It's at its highest here; a great pebble dune rises, in a series of sweeping platforms, some 50 ft (15 m) above sea level at low water. The pebbles are piled up against the contorted cliff face of the Point,[139] brought here by the progressive tidal action known as 'longshore drift.'

[139]*At Hurlstone Point, the upper layers of dull red Hangman sandstone are bent into a dramatic concave shape called 'a syncline.' This rests on horizontal layers of older Devonian sandstones which formed on the beds of ancient rivers. Hangman and all the sandstones of the Exmoor area belong to the Devonian Period, 405 - 355 million years ago.*

The ridge, in this part of the bay, is relatively stable since the large pebbles on the uppermost level are spotted with grey-green lichen - indicating they haven't shifted for some time. Moving westwards along the ridge, you arrive at the point where Horner Water (now including the River Aller) arrives at the shore, having crossed the meadows from Bossington. The river has formed a deep gulley[140] behind the shingle ridge. Here, it flows and pools before disappearing, beneath and through the ridge, unseen into the sea. When the Aller and Horner Water are in full flood, this can form into a substantial lagoon.

Poised on the crest of the shingle is a Second World War pillbox, whose seaward foundations have so worn away, it looks as if it could slip down the slope into the sea. It's built from Porlock Bay pebbles and reminded me of the stone walls at Steart (back along the coast). The pillbox has filled with stones - as though the shingle ridge is reclaiming its own. Close by and set back behind the ridge are the ruins of several big lime-kilns. Unlike most of the kilns along the coastline which are built into a cliff-face, these are free-standing and solidly constructed of pebble sandstone. Facing the sea is the loading ramp and below, on two sides, are brick-arched draw-holes, with the grating, through which the quicklime was extracted, still intact. (See Special Page 'Lime-kilns and Lime'). It's easy to imagine the boats, buttressed with timbers knocked into the beach, pulled up onto the pebble bank with their cargo of culm and limestone. The longshore men would have had to work quickly. North-east winds could make the entire stretch of shingle into a hazardous lee shore (ie. facing the wind) so the boatmen must always have been on watch. A weir-harbour would have made life much safer.

Just west of Horner Water there is a broad track taking you back into Bossington village. When we walked this way in early June, with swallows flying pell-mell along the line of the lane, the hedgerows overflowed with cow parsley and high-standing hogweed pushed above the bracken, their white umbrella flowers busy with insects. Dog roses arched over and through the hedges, cascading drifts of white and blushed flowers, their scent describing all the sweetness of that summer day.

[140]*Once known as 'Haven Pool', the gulley may well have served as a weir-harbour at one time - as at Dunster beach. My 1809 Ordnance map shows a definite breach in the ridge with a small inlet spur leading to the lime-kilns close by.*

Dog rose

The Coastal Path, at one time, had you walking down this way into Bossington before sending the jolly stroller up over Bossington Hill by way of Hurlstone Combe. Odd, since it's quite straightforward along the shingle ridge and up the promontory path. Moving west, we had the choice of a rattley passage along the ridge or, in its lee, a sheltered track by the field margins. Two thirds of the way along the bay we found it's no longer possible to pursue the Coastal Path to Porlock Weir. In 1996 the sea broke through the shore defences, fracturing the ridge to open a muddy canyon and salting the meadows beyond. At low tide, Porlock's stream, Hawkcombe Water, re-emerges from the marshland, to flow briskly to the sea, ignoring the busted conduits of the 1825 'New Works' drainage scheme piled up nearby.

The American War Memorial at Porlock Bay

Backtracking behind the shingle ridge, along the field-way, you come to a touching Second World War memorial[141] of lichened, utilitarian, concrete. The small brass tablet, listing the lost lives, could have been fashioned in a home workshop with a simple letter punch, amplifying its poignancy.

[141]*On October 29th 1942, an American long range Consolidated B-24D Liberator bomber crashed on the Porlock Marsh while returning from antisubmarine patrol in the Bay of Biscay. The plaque reads: P. & D. B. B. LEGION 1945 IN MEMORY OF THESE ELEVEN BRAVE U.S.A. AIRMEN WHO DIED HERE ON OCTOBER TWENTY NINTH. NINETEEN FORTY TWO : L.C.REISS : W.DUFFLEMAN : I.W.LEWIS : W.J.WILLIAMS : J.DIMUZO : E.R.PURDY : J.D.ODELL : C.G.SORRELL : S.D.WARDNEY : J.G.SIMPSON : & : ONE UNKNOWN.*

Near here, Sparkhayes Lane[142] traverses the marshy ground to Porlock. Sea-water has changed things. It's like the set in 'Waiting for Godot.' The saltmarsh grass (Pucinella maritima) is a dull grey-green. Trees stand gaunt and dead against the sky. At one time these fields, or others close by, grew the best barley.[143] The sea's incursions, in the early 1990s, provoked much local controversy (Special Page: 'Porlock Bay and the Shingle Ridge'). A few hundred yards up the lane, the old meadows return with boundary hedges full of songbirds - we heard some fine oratorios from blackbirds and song thrushes. Walking along the main path is discouraged but the field-ways are balmy and easy underfoot. About a mile brought us to Sparkhayes Farm with its splendid campsite and then, almost immediately, into Porlock High Street, opposite the church.

Saltmarsh, Porlock Bay, looking west

[142]*Sparkhayes Lane is quite markedly below the level of the fields it passes between. It has been mooted that the lane may once have been the route of Porlock's main stream to the sea.*

[143]*The Porlock area was noted for the quality of its barley. Bossington, Sparkhayes and Court Place Farms competed against one another for medals and cups, with Sparkhayes winning the World Championship in 1980. Sparkhayes Farm once had its own malt-house - its last malting took place in 1946.*

Porlock Bay and the Shingle Ridge

The wide pebble beach of Porlock Bay (known as the 'shingle ridge')
extends some 3 miles (5 km) westwards, from Hurlstone Point to Gore Point.
For centuries, it has protected the Porlock Marsh from the sea in all but the most violent storms.
The ridge is the product of rock debris, left at the base of Exmoor cliffs at the end of the
last ice-age (10,000 years ago), which then moved eastwards along the coast
as a result of tidal action (longshore drift). In recent times, the integrity of the
ridge appears to have become more vulnerable, and a series of breaches during the 1990s
led to the decision no longer to intervene in its repair.

The weakness of the ridge is probably due to a number of factors:
(i) the supply of rock debris from the Ice-Age is running out;
(ii) man's interference by constructing groynes (especially west of Porlock Weir)
has impoverished the pebble supply to the centre of the beach and altered
inshore wave action; (iii) pebble beaches tend to move inland and,
if situated between headlands, the centre advances more quickly and gets stretched and thinned;
(iv) an increasing frequency of very high tides and a possible rise in sea levels.

Bore holes have shown that the sea has invaded the bay fairly frequently
over the past 6,000 years. From 1824, the construction of groynes and insertion
of a sluice gate in the ridge ('New Works') minimised the salination of the marsh
and created the summer meadows. Since the 1960s various schemes and reports
have promoted a variety of sea-defences, most of which were uneconomic.
Understandably, local people were very unhappy at the prospect of increasing
sea incursion and the loss of pasture. On specialist advice, the National Trust,
which owns Bossington beach (where the pebble build-up is at its highest),
refused removal of shingle for repairs at the central zone. It was felt that the
creation of sea-water lagoons and saltmarsh behind the ridge would slow
and contain tidal breakthrough more effectively.

In November 1995 the District Council, responding to local pressure,
elected to help maintain the ridge. At a meeting on October 18th 1996 there was general
relief because the ridge was "looking very good." 10 days later, south-west gales
(the vestiges of 'Hurricane Lili') veered north-east, hammering the Somerset coast.
Waves overwhelmed the ridge, creating a new channel with large stretches of the
ridge lowered and areas of alluvial clay exposed. Repairs to the ridge were considered
to be impracticable, so a substantial part of the marshland now floods with
every spring tide and saltmarsh is beginning to develop. There is no doubt
that a beautiful environment has been lost, but hopefully what will
emerge will be a new, beneficial and sustainable ecology, with Porlock Bay
safer from being 'injured by the sea.'

Rather than going up Sparkhayes Lane, there is a track westwards, along the edge
of the marsh, to Porlock Weir - now adopted as the re-routed Coastal Path. Here,
single banked hedgerows defend the pasture to the south. On the seaward side,
stretches of hedgerow appear black and gaunt, littered with the stiff stalks of dead
elms. This is an area of ecological revolution and the conversion of pasture to saltmarsh
presents English Nature with a rare opportunity to monitor environmental change.
But it's not pretty.

Close to where the footpath branches off to West Porlock, there stands a small, neat, L-shaped stone barn.[144] A few cast-off farm implements lean against its walls and, curiously, in one of the upper storage bays, the bow of a blue canoe peeks out. In the same field as the barn stand the erect white cadavers of two big oak trees - cut short in their prime. And yet, a few yards away, cattle are grazing on summer meadows and the hedgerows are bursting with life.

[144]*Known locally as the 'Decoy Barn or Coy Barn', a place for storing the decoy netting and frames used to catch wild fowl. The decoy was the pond onto which unfortunate birds (duck, young swans, geese) were lured. From there they were driven down wide net funnels and captured at the narrow end. 'Decoy' is marked on my 1809 map.*

12 noon. Little wind. Motor sailing. Wide brushstrokes of grey pebbles along the shingle ridge of Porlock Bay. The rock stratification practically vertical at Hurlstone Point. Drapery of scree. The Coastguard station. Treeless Hurlstone Combe runs down to Bossington Beach. Westward: the hog's back headlands of Gore, Glenthorne and Foreland Point sniff the shoreline.

Chapter Eighteen

PORLOCK

Porlock churchyard

At the Allerford junction the A39 makes a sharp 90 degree turn and, after a brief
bendy climb, drops abruptly to arrive in Porlock almost by surprise. The village is
gathered into the crook between Crawter and Porlock Hills, below the wooded hamlet
of Hawkcombe whose namesake combe runs up onto Exmoor. For many, Porlock is
the true gateway to the moor, a place of small hotels, and guest-houses offering B&B.
For such a small community, it is blessed with a disproportionate number of good
restaurants and pubs, trekking shops, sweetshops, bookshops and galleries. As yet,
there is no national chain supermarket, which is why so many local stores survive.

Since the early 20th century Porlock's economy has increasingly come to depend on the tourist,[145] and it's for that reason the 'Foot and Mouth' disease outbreak in 2001 was so devastating. Walking the moors and combes was barred, and access to the beaches severely restricted. For a whole season and more, mobility was frozen and many businesses, unable to withstand months of stagnant trade, went to the wall. Farming was profoundly affected. For Porlock, tourism has become a necessary burden and something it struggles to come to terms with.

Despite the A39 crawling through its midst, Porlock retains a kindly and avuncular atmosphere. Although a few thatched originals have been lost along the High Street - many to road widening down the years, it remains pretty hostile to through traffic! But it's easy to escape the press by slipping down Sparkhayes Lane to the sea, or up Parsons Street towards Hawkcombe.

At the heart of the village is St. Dubricius Church, quirky, because it's lost the top of its shingled spire.[146] The church (and Porlock) once belonged to Lady Jane Grey - the 'Nine Days Queen' - who lost her head in 1554 through the political machinations of her father and her husband (who were also beheaded). Her forebears, who kept their heads, John and Elizabeth Harington, lie within the church, beneath their cool, alabaster, simulcra.[147] In the encompassing churchyard, handsome slate gravestones exhibit a surprising verbosity.

[145] *Prior to the holiday business, Porlock depended on farming, fishing and trade through its small weir-port, a bit of smuggling, oysters, a large tannery (closed in 1930), charcoal burning and the production of quicklime. According to local historian Dennis Corner, streams powered many corn and fulling mills - some of which switched to producing electricity at the end of the 19th century.*

[146]*Probably removed by the Great Storm of 1703. St. Dubricius, a Welsh saint, is averred to have crowned King Arthur, officiated at Arthur's wedding to Guinevere and lived happily ever after in Porlock until aged 150 or so. He died around 550 AD.*

[147]*Close to, the effigies are intriguingly scarred with medieval graffiti - some dated as far back as 1640. The fevered scratchings even course their way across the courtly cheeks and foreheads.*

Often quoted, but irresistible, are the lines for Thomas and Prudence Rawle:

"He first departed,
she for one day tried
to live without him,
liked it not, and dy'd."

Directly opposite the church gates, on the High street, is an elongated and becoming thatched building which goes back to 1624 or so. This is 'The Rose and Crown, a former inn where R.D.Blackmore stayed while working on Lorna Doone in the 1860s. Later, it became a bank and a shop, and is now two houses.

Doverhay Forge

Rosie and I walked up the Doverhay, a road from the High Street leading uphill and due south towards Hawkcombe hamlet. At the entrance to the road stands Dovery Manor; a 15th century dower house rescued and restored by Charles Chadwyck

Doverhay Farm

Healey[148] in 1895. It is now the village's museum. Almost immediately, on the left hand side, are the red doors of the long established Doverhay Forge, while to the right is a path, curiously called 'The Drang,'[149] which led us between cottages and gardens towards the church. This is a lovely part of the village, but it's not that long ago a thatched house was demolished to make way for a car-park. Further up the Doverhay is a group of 17th century thatched buildings, of which Doverhay House is the main component. They are especially attractive, having had the same 'cottage orne' makeover as the buildings on Selworthy Green in the early 19th century. Another 400 yards (366 m) and we arrived at the Higher[150] and Lower Doverhay Farms most of whose land has either been built upon or sold. The Higher Farm (now called simply 'Doverhay Farm') has so far held onto some surrounding pastureland. It remains a typical 'longhouse' building of great charm; at one time, people and cattle would have been housed under its single roof, separated by a 'cross-passage.' One way of keeping warm.

[148]*An enlightened act of local philanthropy. Healey wrote the extraordinary 'History of the Part of West Somerset' which describes the family stories of the Porlock area.*

[149]*Same Old English origin as 'drong,' meaning a narrow passageway.*

[150]*Charles Harper describes a smuggler's hiding-hole discovered at Higher Doverhay Farm - "an ingenious place of concealment." A false wall had been constructed leaving a narrow space with shelves to hold the brandy-kegs. At the time of discovery the kegs had been spirited away...*

Beyond the farmhouses, the road divides around an area of pasture with an elderly Ferguson tractor languishing inside the farm gate. The Hawkcombe road passes above Porlock's cemetery where a wicket gate reveals a beautiful view across the gravestones and the Recreation Ground, to Porlock and the sea. From the gate, steps lead down into the well-tended graveyard, past a sign announcing:

Out to grass

Having crossed the path between the graves, we arrived at another sign by the lychgate, similar to the first, but adding: *"No Horses."* The notices seem to work. We came across not a single person, child, horse or dog carrying wood.

The stream from Hawk Combe (Hawkcombe Water) runs around the western side of the cemetery, before emerging from its ferny dell and alongside Parson Street. Following the stream up into the combe brought us to the hamlet, Hawkcombe, with its orderly terraces of Victorian cottages lined up against the hillside. These once housed the families of the workmen who had laboured in the quarries[151] and tree plantations of the surrounding combes (which explains the "no wood carrying" edict). The track follows the course of Hawkcombe Water through dense coppiced oak woodland,[152] passing houses that in winter must receive little sunlight.

Hawkcombe

[151]*Much of Porlock's building stone came from here - Old Red Sandstone.*

[152]*The Sessile oak (Quercus petraea) tolerates the acidic Exmoor soil. Coppicing involved the felling of the trees to ground level and the resulting ring of smaller trunk regrowth gathered in cycles of 10 - 20 years. These were then stripped of their bark, to be used in Porlock's leather tannery, and the wood for posts, fuel anqd especially charcoal. Some bark was exported. The Tannery operated for some hundreds of years and once employed over 30 men. It closed around 1930.*

A mile or so up the combe the trees fall back a little, to reveal a handsome but simple Georgian house, with the dainty name 'Peep-out.' Its close neighbour, a Victorian lodge built in a Bavarian style, we were told once housed hunting parties. Back in Hawkcombe, the road returns to Porlock down Parson Street passing the Hawkcombe Mill,[153] set back hard into the side of the lower combe. The waterwheel still turns on occasions but these days produces no power.

One of the really delicious things about Porlock is the pervasive smell of roasting coffee.[154] D.J. Miles, Tea & Coffee Merchants, have their premises just off the High Street. Derek Miles's grandfather began tea blending in Birmingham, in 1888. Derek opened his own shop in Minehead in 1961, moving the main business to Porlock a few years later. Equally evocative is The Ship Inn, just on the turnoff for Porlock Hill. Its high chimney has a laconic lean and the pub rooms hold onto an atmosphere which evokes the Romantic Poets[155] who passed this way in the late 1800s.

[153]*The mill belonged to the Rectory Manor and ground Porlock's corn for hundreds of years. In 1911 it became the village's first electricity supplier and continued to do so until 1932.*

[154]*It reminds me of the 1960s, in Weston-super-Mare, when the flaming coffee drums revolved in the shop-windows of Lyons and Carwardines; blue scented smoke billowing into the High Street.*

[155]*Coleridge and Wordsworth must have rested here on their various pilgrimages. Their friend Robert Southey, escaping "unwelcome summer rain," found the time to compose:*

"Porlock, thy verdant vale, so fair to sight,
Thy lofty hill, which fern and furze embrown,
Thy waters, that roll musically down
Thy woody glens, the traveller with delight
Recalls to memory, and the channel grey
Circling its surges in thy level bay.

Porlock, I also shall forget thee not,
Here by the unwelcome summer rain confined;
But often shall hereafter call to mind
How here, a patient prisoner, 't was my lot
To wear the lonely, lingering close of day,
Making my Sonnet by the alehouse fire,
Whilst Idleness and Solitude inspire
Dull rhymes to pass the duller hours away."

August 1799.

The Ship Inn

When Paul Tregunna and I pedalled through Porlock in the late 1950s, we had heard of the infamous 'Hill' and its 1:4 gradient. We didn't pedal up very far, what with loaded panniers and all. So it was a long push. Back in 1909, Charles Harper described the three mile climb, with some consternation, as "the worst hill in the West of England... in summer a mass of red dust six or eight inches deep and plentifully mixed with large stones, it is in winter a pudding-like mixture of a clayey nature." He was astonished and anxious about the teams of horses that hauled the heavy laden stagecoaches up the hill. Indeed, coming down was even more hazardous. Harper reckoned you'd have to be a madman to attempt riding down on a bike.[156] In 1959, we went home by another way.

[156]*There are easier ways, both toll roads. The 'New Road' (1869) starts soon after the main road junction and ascends, by a gentle incline, through the wooded estates above West Porlock. The other begins at Worthy, west of Porlock Weir, running up Worthy Combe to the A39 on Culbone Hill. The Porlock Hill stagecoaches kept going until 1920.*

Clotted Cream

"Clowted crayme and rawe crayme, put together, is eaten more for a sensuall apptyte than for any good nouryshment". So spake Andrew Boorde in 1542. The first person I saw making clotted cream was Gladys Tregunna, mother of Paul, a school-friend - and Cornish to boot! She would place rich, creamy, milk in a wide deep pan and then warm it through on a low heat, until the milk began to skin and crinkle. Gladys called this 'scalding'. She would then remove the pan from the heat, cover with a cloth and allow it to cool and rest for 24 hours. In that time the 'clotts' would have formed a 1" thick (or more) golden buttery crust which she would gently ladle out. We would have it with fresh bread and raspberry jam. A 'clowt' or 'clout' means 'the patch' - the thick crust - that forms on the top of the milk.

and a big dollop of clotted cream ...

As well as having its own special, luxurious, texture, it must have been an effective early form of pasteurisation which would keep the cream sweet for a good time. The layers of cream were often 'Swiss-rolled', with sugar and rose water sprinkled in between, and served with ginger or nutmeg. For me, it's wonderful with strawberries or black and red currant pie, made with my mum's sweet short-crust pastry.

Apparently the AA and RAC once kept barrels of water on the hill so motorists could refill their boiling radiators. The AA 'telephone box no. 137' still stands on the A39 at Pittcombe Head, and is now a listed building! A short distance from the telephone box brings you to the turnoff for Oare, a steep minor road that takes you deep into Doone Country. Straightaway you enter the Lorna Doone saga by crossing 'Robber's Bridge' where the father of John Ridd (the story's protagonist) was murdered. The tale reaches its climax, in the tiny village of Oare, a few miles further along the road. The whitewashed church of St. Mary[157] was the scene for Carver Doone's shooting of Lorna, at her wedding to John Ridd. Carver took aim through one of the single-light windows at the side of the old chancel. Two centuries ago, Oare was at the edge of the civilised world with St. Mary's serving a remote and isolated community. Not surprising since they'd have had to pedal up Porlock Hill.

[157]*Author R.D. Blackmore was the grandson of John Blackmore, Rector of Oare from 1809 to 1842.*

Chapter Nineteen

PORLOCK WEIR TO GLENTHORNE

Turkey Cottages, Porlock Weir

At the western extremity of Porlock Bay, beneath 'the hanging woods' of the
Exmoor escarpment, lies the secretive haven of Porlock Weir. The gentle descent
from Porlock eases through the hillside hamlet of West Porlock, the high elm hedgerows
latticed with field maple, sessile oak and ash, punctuated every few hundred yards by
wide, wind-shaped oaks and dying elms.[158] The fields fall away to the sea. The wind
feels softer here.

[158]*Dutch Elm disease is still very active since it arrived in
England from America in the 1970s. The English elm survives in its hedge
form but once it gains tree size it is vulnerable to beetle and fungal attack.*

There's a moderate rise into West Porlock; an attractive mixture of 1920's houses with terraced gardens and cottages presses against the roadside, but the road soon dips again, trees crowding in on the hillside slopes. Here, dominated by great Monterey pines, the road divides, the upper road (the original way to 'The Weir'), signposted for Worthy, Ashley Combe and Lynmouth.

The lower road, the 'new' entrance into the village, makes a final dip towards the sea and, rounding the corner, arrives at the westmost limit of the shingle ridge.[159] We are back on Porlock Bay. From here, the village must look much as it did 100 years ago: the cluster of Gibraltar cottages crouched on the shoreline, their gardens merging into the pebbles; the huge palisade of groynes defending the harbour entrance and, surmounting the jetty wall, another group of cottages called Turkey, with the Union Jack flying boldly above them.

[159]*The beach road was constructed, along with a new sea-wall, in 1894.*
Prior to that there was just a track along the shingle ridge.
It made it possible for houses to be built facing the sea.

2 pm. We carried on with the tide to Glenthorne and then moored
off Porlock Weir for lunch. Harbour buildings concealed by the shingle ridge.
We can make out the flag flying above Turkey Cottages.
Looks sheltered and warm. Trees crowd down to the shoreline.
Waiting for the tide to turn before heading back home.

When I used to come here on family 'outings,' the present car-park was just a rough patch of ground where Dad would draw up in the Austin 16. Well before that, it was the site of the Weir fish-market and besides herring, mackerel and cod, there was a good trade in oysters.[160] The small port is that rare thing; a functioning 'weir-harbour,' already described in a footnote in the Dunster chapter. Maintaining the breach through the shingle ridge was always a problem - partly achieved by damming the waters behind sluice gates which, when opened, scoured 'the guts' (ie. the channel) of mud and pebbles. These days, the gates have fallen into disuse and the channel is kept clear by mechanical diggers.

To reach Turkey Cottages, a narrow metal bridge crosses the harbour entrance above the redundant sluice gates. With their thatched and tiled roofs, these are Porlock Weir's landmark buildings. They are the ones that give the harbour its particular shape. Like Gibraltar cottages, they sit just behind the crest of the shingle ridge, which here, by means of ranked groynes, rises some 45 ft (14 m) above the harbour channel at low water. The cottages are built from large beach stones, with traditional cob[161] walling at the higher levels. They may well be over 600 years old. On the seaward side of the cottages, a Second World War pillbox (identical to the one close to the Porlock Bay lime kilns) is tipped at a precarious angle and, like its fellow, seems it could just slide into the sea at any moment.

Beyond the sluice gates lies 'the dock' - the inner harbour. By the early 1900s, much of this area had filled up with wrecks and rotting hulks, so much so it got to be called 'the graveyard.' In 1913, the whole lot was cleared out and new sluice gates fitted. Sadly, despite this investment, the small-craft shipping trade continued to decline and, with the disappearance of the herring, fishing too faded away.

[160] According to marine historian Brian Waters, up to 1910 the Perkins family (and the Pollards) had three oyster dredgers based at the Weir, harvesting the shellfish from a rich bed between Porlock and Lynmouth; "somewhere around the 10 fathom mark off the Exmoor coast." The oysters were brought back to harbour and kept alive in a seaside pool (called 'a perch') a short distance off the beach road.

[161] 'Cob;' an ancient building material, was made primarily of clay and straw, but often with mud, dung, animal hair and lime thrown in. Limewashed, it is long-lasting, weatherproof and snug.

Close to the dock area, on its landward side, is a large stone building, now a private residence, which was once the Weir's lime kiln[162] (see Special Page on 'Lime'). An important part of the port's trade was the limestone and culm imported from South Wales to be burnt in the kilns. The resulting lime was used to 'sweeten' Exmoor's acidic soil.

[162]*Exmoor historian John Gilman tells the story of Farmer John Redd of Broomstreet Farm,
west of Culbone, who, around 1900, built a lime kiln on the beach to which he cut
a formidable 1000 ft (300m) zigzag track, down through the coastal woodland.
The first consignment of limestone and culm was unloaded onto the beach,
hauled over the rocks to the kiln and burned.
They then had to transport the quicklime up the steep twisting track to the moor.
And that was it. Once was enough. Never again. Farmer John was also
responsible for many of the wrecks that filled up the inner harbour -
he couldn't resist a bargain.
One of the boats he bought, that managed to stay afloat, was apparently
"a bit like sailing a haystack."
He was a great character and the tales about him are legion.*

Facing the south-west jetty wall stands The Ship, a hostelry long famed for its maritime connections and often confused with its sister establishment back in Porlock. Poets aplenty must have mused here too and it's an important component of the Weir's picturesque scene. In winter months a wonderful log fire burns in its wide fireplace. But, inevitably perhaps, it's losing out to tripperdom - my impression, undoubtedly coloured by an expensive 'open crab sandwich' on our last visit, which would have been best left closed. Shame that.

Above the west wall of the outer harbour stands a handsome, three-storey, dormer-windowed building in red sandstone. Now called The Pieces of Eight, it was once a grocery and a grain store and has become, at ground level, a cafe and shops selling seasidey things. Running behind The Pieces of Eight is a lane which leads to the dock, with several single-storey workshops (former stables) set against the hill. One of these houses 'Exmoor Glass,' where we were captured by the sight of roaring furnaces and craftsmen spinning and blowing great globs of glowing, molten, glass. Next door, a blacksmith hammers his trade and a little further stands the former lime-kiln in its dwelling-house disguise.

The dock is well filled by motor cruisers and yachts. At low water, it's pebble-bottomed, with a gentle incline to the west. The mouldering hulks (which might have belonged to Farmer John Redd) and a Huckleberry Finn houseboat, lend a romantic piquancy to the scene. And there does seem to be some professional fishing going on - we came upon a scatter of lobster and crab pots along the harbour wall. But I'm unconvinced they had anything to do with the contents of my 'open crab sandwich.'

The 'old' road into the village arrives just east of The Ship. On its way, it passes a delightful white 'tin church' - St. Nicholas Chapel - built of corrugated iron sheets.[163] Along the same road, set back against the hill, above a tall stone wall, is a long, mostly thatched, high-chimneyed terrace known as Lane Head Cottages.[164] Opposite, fields slope down to the shore. These are much the same age as Turkey and Gibraltar cottages but built in a rather more sensible position, secure from sea invasion.

Across Porlock Bay, from Worthy

[163] *These 'tin churches' were designed in Victorian times, amongst the first prefabricated buildings. They were much used in the 'days of Empire.'*

[164] *Also called 'Beelzebub Terrace.' John Gilman relates queer happenings and hauntings occurring here, down the years.*

The South West Coast Path, thwarted by the breach in the shingle ridge (it had to cross Porlock Bay a short distance inland, behind the saltmarsh), finds its way back to the shore at Porlock Weir. Rosie and I picked it up where it climbs behind The Anchor Hotel and on, along the edge of open pasture, above the inner harbour. In mid-April, the fields were full of bouncing lambs feverishly racing from one hedgerow to another. A short distance brought us to a point where the fields and woods meet and the track joins the narrow tarmac road to Worthy. Looking back, the scene was like an idyll: hedgerows in fresh new leaf and the bright greens of spring grass, the faded red-grey of the shoreline and the grey-green sea arcing, eastwards, to the hazy promontory of Hurlstone Point below Bossington Hill.

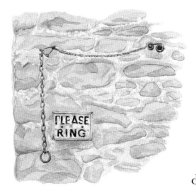

The road halts at an elegantly curved, thatched, gatehouse - once the entrance to Ashley Combe House,[165] which no longer exists. The gatehouse has two brick archways; one permits, for a small toll, entrance to the Worthy Combe[166] road, for this is the other way of avoiding Porlock Hill. The second arch allows passage to the coastal path for Culbone. Both entrances have white gates and there's a bell-pull which dangles like a lavatory chain and begs; "Please Ring."

On the wall above the path gate is a small notice board listing the times and dates of services at Culbone church and also St. Mary's church at Oare. It's curious, but at some time in the recent past Ashley has become Worthy Combe. Despite the signpost at the entrance to Porlock Weir stating the contrary. I wonder why?

[165] *Built in 1799, in an Italianate style, complete with a campanile clock-tower it lorded the hillside above Porlock Weir. It was owned by the Lovelace family and during much of its latter days was let to hunting parties. Sadly it fell into disuse and disrepair and, during the peculiar economics of the 1960s, was demolished. Many country houses were lost during this time. Charles Harper considered it "beautifully placed and finely appointed".*

[166] *The house called Worthy Manor, lying below the gatehouse towards the sea, was never a manorial estate - it was part of the manor of Porlock. But the building, though part 'modern', goes back to the mid-17th century at least. (C. Chadwyck Healey)*

The path now enters what is probably the longest stretch of coastal woodland in the British Isles.[167] Almost immediately, it becomes dense and dark with a gloomy evergreen under-canopy of Holm oak and laurel and the strange tunnels[168] of the departed Ashley Combe estate. Ascending, the gloom quickly disperses as light-leafed birches take over alongside the grassy zigzag path. Then on through coppiced oak and sycamore, by-passing places where the old way has disappeared through landslip and tree-fall. Sometimes this involves short steep climbs up steps cut into the hillside, at others, more circuitous detours above the areas of collapse.

Rosie and I walked this track in April and June. During spring, the tree cover was in young leaf, and we could see as well as hear the green-blue sea rattling at the cliffs below us. In summer the waves were mostly unseen, just occasional sightings where a fallen tree had torn a hole in the curtain. It's extraordinary that, on such steep and fragile terrain, trees could take hold and survive at all. At times the cliffs fall almost sheer to the sea, but still the trees hang on.

After a few miles above the shoreline, the trail, deep with tall sweet chestnuts, oaks and sycamores, curves inland into Culbone Combe. On both days we were there, we arrived just before noon, the sun slanting straight down the valley. The first sight of the small church is always unexpected: glimpsed between the trees, low down on the combe floor, standing clear of the surrounding woodland, the flaking limewash white-grey in the morning sunlight.

[167]*Samuel Coleridge, with William and Dorothy Wordsworth, came this way in late 1797*
on their journey to North Devon's 'Valley of the Rocks,'
and Coleridge was to do it again the following June with William Hazlitt.
Indeed it seems likely Coleridge walked this track many times.

[168]*Local legend has it the tunnels allowed tradesmen and their vehicles to*
approach the house without offending the view.

The church at Culbone

Despite its seclusion, St. Beuno's Church[169] has been a place of modest pilgrimage for centuries. It has the restorative quietude and simplicity of a retreat. As we descended the combe's eastern side, the church remained elusive, never quite showing itself completely, until we came to the sloping valley floor. The Culbone stream tumbles down the hillside from somewhere up above, passes below the churchyard wall on the east side and then tumbles on to the sea. Other than the church, there are a few tidy stone farm-buildings (early 20th century) and particularly, a cedar hut where, in the spirit of the place, the Culbone Trust offers 'Refreshments' for whatever you can afford.

[169]It's likely Culbone derived from two Celtic words, 'Kil Beun,' meaning simply the Church of St. Beuno. Its ancient name was Kitnor which, in Saxon, meant 'a cave by the sea.' Beuno was a Welsh saint, bravely active in the dangerous days of the 7th century, defending the Christian faith. Like St. Decuman of Watchet, he was useful in instances of decapitation - several murdered Christians were grateful to him for reattaching their heads. Harper has a different explanation saying that Culbone was a corruption of 'Columban,' St. Columban being a 6th century saint, but Irish this time. He apparently was of "a respectable family" but lacked recapitation credentials.

St. Beuno's is famously 'the smallest parish church in England,' measuring 35 ft. (10.6 m) long internally with 2 ft. (0.6 m) thick, rubble stone walls. It has a tiny spire which some have claimed to be the storm-detatched cap of Porlock's steeple. Would it were so! Inside an unadorned solemnity greeted us, the air cool and clear, contrasting with the warm June sun outside. High on the west wall hung Nicholas Red's (churchwarden 1836) dolorous transcription of the Ten Commandments, which spoilt things a bit. But Gerald Harper loved this place and wrote simply "It is like the peace of God."[170]

Beehive

Outside the mood prevailed. We sat on a small terrace above the churchyard, birds came and perched in the shrubs around us, then accompanied us as we explored the churchyard, flying from gravestone to gravestone. The first time this happened it was a joyful experience, when it happened the second time it was an affirmation.

A short distance above the church the combe divides, with Culbone Combe continuing to the south and Withy Combe to the south-west. Ash Farm lies close to Culbone Combe and may have been where Coleridge was disturbed from his opium reverie[171] by "the person on business from Porlock," thus consigning much of the poetic fragment 'Kubla Khan' to oblivion.[172] The way now returns to the cliff-path ascending on the west side of the combe, St. Beuno's slipping swiftly behind the trees. The Somerset - Devon border is now only a few miles away and this part of the journey is something of a Grand Finale.

[170]*Culbone does have its dark side. In the 13th century it was marked as a place of banishment , and a hundred years later it became a prison colony. In 1544 that changed to a leper settlement for 45 men, women and children living off the land and the woods. Barred from contact with the outside world, the lepers were not allowed to enter the church - a small 'leper squint' window was the only access to the services. The last leper died in 1622. In the early 18th century, 38 French prisoners-of-war were sent to Culbone, where they became charcoal burners and oak bark gatherers.*

[171]*Coleridge wrote;"In consequence of a slight indisposition, an anodyne had been prescribed..."*

[172]*In Coleridge's time there was also a farm up Withy Combe. Indeed it is there on my 1809 map and a marked trail runs down to the church. Tom Mayberry has raised the reasonable speculation that Withycombe Farm was more likely to have been Coleridge's boarding-house - it was nearer and more direct.*

Coast path to Silcombe

The Coast Path runs along the Exmoor cliffs at about 650 to 1000 feet (200 - 300m) above the sea. Combes arrive nearly every half-mile with the way turning inland for a short time to cross another splashing brook dancing down to the Severn Sea. Withy Combe, Silcombe Combe, Holmer's Combe, Twitchin Combe, Broomstreet Combe,[173] Wheatham Combe... In April, with the tree canopy letting the sun through in bright shafts, each combe was a dancing interplay of light and water. The trunks of fallen trees were covered in ferns and thick, luminous, moss. The lime-green flowers of small euphorbias, picked out in splashes of sunlight, competed for attention with the delicate, white, wood-sorrel. It was so astonishingly beautiful.

---

[173]*Broomstreet Combe accommodates Broomstreet Farm where Farmer John Redd lived. Presumably the twisting track from the farm, through Embelle Wood, to Embelle Beach was the route that broke his lime production ambitions. The farm is also on the list of possible Coleridge biding places.*

This Somerset journey is coming to an end, rattling off one combe after another. A coda of combes. The path arrives at Wheatham Combe at an altitude of 1,000 ft (300m) to descend the slopes of Sugarloaf Hill into Yenworthy Wood. Here the tree cover is lighter, allowing grass to grow alongside the track, as it makes its way on down into Yenworthy Combe.[174] We arrived at the Yenworthy stream, easily crossed, to come to a small metal gate which allows access to the Glenthorne Estate.

The estate and its inspirationally placed house was the lifework of the Rev. Walter Halliday during the early 19th century (see Special Page - 'The House at Coscombe'). The house and its grounds were built bestriding the Somerset - Devonshire boundary, which weaves up from the beach, following the inclined combe floor of Coscombe.

[174]The 1809 map shows Yenworthy as Yannery, and Silcombe Combe as Zealcombe.

Ash Farm · Culbone · Withy Combe · Silcombe Combe · Holmers Combe · Twitchin Combe · Pirsomstreet Combe · Wheatham Combe · Glenthorne

Porpoises off Culbone

12.45 pm. A succession of luxuriant wooded combes come down to the water's edge, thinning above as the upper slopes turn to moorland. Glenthorne House perched on a rocky shelf behind its Stone pine. Coscombe swings east and then west between Somerset and Devon. We head back to Porlock Weir where we'll wait for the tide to help us home. Suddenly a school of porpoises are with us, flashes of black and silver breaking the surface. Within a moment they are gone.

The House at Coscombe

Glenthorne from the sea

Glenthorne is a dramatic and romantic house
built on a high sea-bluff at the mouth of
Coscombe, overlooking the Severn Sea.
The Somerset - Devon border runs up the combe
and the house actually stands, just, in Somerset's
sister county. At its zenith, the estate ran to
6,000 acres (2,400 hectares), some of which lay
in Somerset (Yenworthy and Oareford) but
mostly in Devon, taking in the whole parish of
Countisbury, from the Culbone parish boundary
to the hamlet of Countisbury itself.

Severely infected by the Romantic Movement,
the Rev. Walter Halliday arrived at Coscombe in
1829 and, perched on a stone (from then on
called 'The Decision Stone') decided to buy the combe and build a house on a cliff at its mouth
(he just happened to be building a house on a cliff in Lynmouth at the time). It took a year to cut
and lay the 3 mile (5 km) carriageway to the site together with a small quay, storerooms for coal
and a lime kiln on the beach. The house is built of red sandstone with Bath stone detailing.
In her book 'Glenthorne,' Ursula Halliday describes it as being "Gothicised Georgian-Tudor,"
comfortable and homely in scale, anticipating the Victorian villa. The house's design, together
with its accompanying Lodge and Home Farm buildings, was hugely influenced by the romantic
ideas of philosopher Uvedale Price and architect P.F. Robinson.
And, of course, Coleridge and Wordsworth had just happened to have passed this way.

Walter constructed an icehouse, fish ponds, fish weirs, scenic walkways, planted gardens
and a pine wood (including the commanding Stone pine on the seaward side of the house)
and a conservatory, and extended the house and the estate in various ways. He called it
Glenthorne (not at all West country), acknowledging his Scottish roots. He delighted in
entertaining innumerable guests, both family and friends, and showing off his home with its
matchless outlook. He appears to have been a determined but gentle and kind man. He died,
aged 78, in 1872, painlessly, from a chill. The house remained in family ownership until 1984.

Back at the metal gate, the trail divides, with the left path ascending the Somerset side of Coscombe, through beautiful woodland, to emerge on Exmoor close to the County Gate. The right-hand path courses downhill, through the pine wood, following the direction of the Yenworthy stream. In summer, the tree canopy becomes quite dense here, the stream catching only momentary splashes of sunlight. In one place, the water has been dammed forming a vitrescent, overhung, pool. Further down, signs led us to Glenthorne's icehouse, a cemented chamber, cut into a high bank, close to the stream.

The path now divides again and, quite suddenly, from behind the trees, we could hear waves working at the shore. The left way, west, brought us to a field of llamas (who seemed as surprised as we were), separating us from the house, its roofs and chimneys just visible amongst the trees. Going right and north, we renewed our companionship with the Yenworthy stream - here cut and channelled alongside the track. Very soon, the narrow road, arriving at the cliff-edge, makes a sharp right-angle down to the beach, while the stream, culverted beneath the path, presses straight on, to leap from darkness into space, dashing itself onto the rocks below.

We walked slowly down the last few yards and arrived at a small quay, now raised only a few feet above the pebble beach. Set back into the cliff face were the remains of a lime-kiln, old store rooms and cellars. Much of what came to be Glenthorne must have come this way.

It was low water and the beach shelved steeply to the green sea. We had an hour before the tide turned and, hoping to get a view of the house, picked our way, westwards, across clattering red-grey pebbles. The Yenworthy stream broke cover from a gulley jammed with bleached and broken trees, splashed the beach and disappeared. Close by came the Coscombe water. At the crook of a rocky promontory below the house, it had carved a groove for itself. With a final, gently interrupted cascade, it too vanished beneath the pebbles. From the water's edge, we could see Walter Halliday's proud Stone pine, but Glenthorne - so close at hand - remained hidden above the bluff.

Eastward from Glenthorne Beach

    Looking east, soft wooded slopes curved gently down to the beaches below Yenworthy and Embelle Woods. Through a heat-haze, we could just make out Hurlstone Point, on the very edge of visibility. But beyond, whatever might have been seen of the West Somerset Coast, had slipped into the mist.

EPILOGUE

The hill still holds the morning's translucence,
Green and brown merging, forming a quiet solidity.
I stand amongst the sea-rubbish
And walk a bit along the shoreline.

Then, sitting, taking it all in,
A wind itches a little, I throw a pebble
And move back with a load of old wood
And pockets full of stones.

BIBLIOGRAPHY

Allen, N. & Giddens, C. 1994, Exploring the Quantock Hills with Chris Chapman
Arend, C. van den & Clinker, C.R. 1986, The West Somerset Railway
Ashford, Philip, 2001, The Port of Porlock Weir 1540 - 1830
Atkinson, Michael (editor), 1997, Exmoor's Industrial Archaeology
Blyton, Enid, 1950, The Mystery of the Invisible Thief
Bird, Eric & Modlock, Lilian, 1994, Writers on the South-West Coast
Bush, Robin, 1994, Somerset. The Complete Guide
Central Electricity Generating Board, 1984, Hinkley Point Nuclear Power Station
Chadwyck Healey, Charles E.H. 1901, The History of the Part of West Somerset
Collings, A.G. 1985, Along the South West Way, Part 1
Concannon, Bernard, 1995, The History of Dunster Beach
Corner, Dennis, 1999, The Book of Porlock
Dunning, Bob, 1992, Bridgwater, History and Guide
Dunning, R.W. Victoria County History Vol. VI, St. Decuman's inc. Watchet & Williton
Edwards, R.A. 2000, Exmoor Geology
Exmoor National Park, 1993, Porlock Village Walks. 1996, Coastal Walks
Evans, I.O. 1952, The Obsever's Book of British Geology
Farr, Grahame, 1954, Somerset Harbours
Fitzhugh, Rod, 1993, Bridgwater and the River Parrett in Old Photographs
Gilman, John, 1999, Exmoor's Maritime History
Greswell, William, 1903, The Land of Quantock
Halliday, Ursula, 1995, Glenthorne - A Most Romantic Place
Hardy, Peter, 1999, The Geology of Somerset
Harper, Charles G. 1909, The Somerset Coast
Hesp, Peter, 1993, Exmoor and West Somerset Coastline
Jackman, Joan, 1999, Brean - The Millennium Years
Johnson, Bill, (editor), 2000, Otterhampton Parish 2000
Jones, R. 1999, West Somerset Railway Guide
Kemm, William St J. The Story of Berrow and Brean
Kille, Herbert W. 2002, The Minehead Hobby-Horse
King, Andrew, 1997, Fossil Ammonites from the Somerset Coast
Lawrence, Berta, 1952, Quantock Country
Layley, Charles G. 1985, St. Beuno's, Culbone
Maslen, G. & Cavell, H. 1990, Around Burnham-on-Sea and Highbridge in Old Photos
Mayberry, Tom, 1992, Coleridge and Wordsworth in the West Country
McTernan, M. & Wilson, H. 1999, Coastal Management in Porlock Bay
Monks, N. & Palmer, P. 2002, Ammonites
National Trust, Holnicote Walks
Newman, Paul, 1976, Channel Passage
Norman, W.H.(Ben), 1988, Tales of Watchet Harbour
Pearce, Brian, 2001, Minehead - A Photographic History
Pevsner, Nikolaus, 1958, South and West Somerset
Riley, Hazel & Wilson-North, Robert, 2001, The Field Archaeology of Exmoor
Sellick, R. J. 1981, The Old Mineral Line
Smith, Samuel, 1994, Three Weeks in Watchet
Somerset Federation of Women's Institutes, 1988, The Somerset Village Book
Waite, Vincent, 1964, Portrait of the Quantocks
Webb, Jeanne, 1995, A Tapestry of Old Cleeve
Waters, Brian, 1955, The Bristol Channel
Williams, Richard, 1989, Lime Kilns and Limeburning